MARRIAGE, AS IT WAS, AS IT IS, AND AS IT SHOULD BE

MARRIAGE, AS IT WAS, AS IT IS, AND AS IT SHOULD BE

BY
ANNIE BESANT

GYAN

ISBN: 978-81-212-1908-2 (HB)
First Published, 1879
Published, 2018
Published by

Gyan Publishing House
5, Ansari Road
Daryaganj, New Delhi-110002
Phone: 011-47034999, 9811692060
www.gyanbooks.com
E-mail: books@gyanbooks.com

Printed at: G. Print Process, Delhi.

MARRIAGE:

AS IT WAS, AS IT IS, AND AS IT SHOULD BE.

"Either all human beings have equal rights, or none have any."—CONDORCET.

THE recognition of human rights may be said to be of modern growth, and even yet they are but very imperfectly understood. Liberty used to be regarded as a privilege bestowed, instead of as an inherent right; rights of classes have often been claimed: right to rule, right to tax, right to punish, all these have been argued for and maintained by force; but these are not rights, they are only wrongs veiled as legal rights. Jean Jacques Rousseau struck a new note when he cried: "Men are born free;" free by birthright was a new thought, when declared as a universal inheritance, and this "gospel of Jean Jacques Rousseau" dawned on the world as the sun-rising of a glorious day—a day of human liberty, unrestrained by class. In 1789 the doctrine of the "Rights of Man" received its first European sanction by law; in the August of that year the National Assembly of France proclaimed: "Men are born, and remain, free and equal in rights . . . . The aim of political association is the conservation of the natural and imprescriptible rights of man; these rights are—liberty, property, safety, and resistance of tyranny." During savage and semi-civilised ages these "imprescriptible rights" are never dreamed of as existing; brute force is king; might is the only right, and the strong arm is the only argument whose logic meets with general recognition. In warlike tribes fair equality is found, and the chief is only *primus inter pares;* but when the nomadic tribe settles down into an agricultural community, when the habit of bearing arms ceases to be universal, when wealth begins to accumulate, and the village or town offers attractions for pillage, then strength becomes at once a terror and a possible defence. The weak obey some powerful neighbour partly because they cannot resist, and partly because they desire, by their submission, to gain a strong protection against their enemies. They submit to the exactions of one that they may be shielded from the tyranny of many, and yield up their natural liberty to some extent to preserve themselves from being entirely enslaved. Very slowly do they learn that the union of many individually feeble is stronger than a few powerful, isolated tyrants, and gradually law takes the place of despotic will; gradually the feeling of self-respect, of independence, of love of liberty, grows, until at last man claims freedom as of right, and denies the authority of any to rule him without his own consent.

Thus the Rights of Man have become an accepted doctrine, but, unfortunately, they are only rights of *man*, in the exclusive sense of the word. They are sexual, and not human rights, and until they become human rights, society will never rest on a sure, because just, foundation. Women, as well as men, "are born and remain free and equal in rights:" women, as well as men, have "natural and imprescriptible rights;" for women, as well as for men, "these rights are—liberty, property, safety, and resistance of tyranny." Of these rights only crime should deprive them, just as by crime men also are deprived of them; to deny these rights to women, is either to deny them to humanity *quâ* humanity, or to deny that women form a part of humanity; if women's rights are denied, men's rights have no logical basis, no claim to respect; then tyranny ceases to be a crime, slavery is no longer a scandal; "either all human beings have equal rights, or none have any."

Naturally, in the savage state, women shared the fate of the physically weak, not only because, as a rule, they are smaller-framed and less muscular than their male comrades, but also because the bearing and suckling of children is a drain on their physical resources from which men are exempt. Hence she has suffered from "the right of the strongest," even more than has man, and her exclusion from all political life has prevented the redressal which man has wrought out for himself; while claiming freedom for himself he has not loosened her chains, and while striking down his own tyrants, he has maintained his personal tyranny in the home. Nor has this generally been done by deliberate intention: it is rather the survival of the old system, which has only been abolished so slowly as regards men. Mrs. Mill writes: "That those who were physically weaker should have been made legally inferior, is quite conformable to the mode in which the world has been governed. Until very lately, the rule of physical strength was the general law of human affairs. Throughout history, the nations, races, classes, which found themselves strongest, either in muscles, in riches, or in military discipline, have conquered and held in subjection the rest. If, even in the most improved nations, the law of the sword is at last discountenanced as unworthy, it is only since the calumniated eighteenth century. Wars of conquest have only ceased since democratic revolutions began. The world is very young, and has only just begun to cast off injustice. It is only now getting rid of negro slavery. It is only now getting rid of monarchical despotism. It is only now getting rid of hereditary feudal nobility. It is only now getting rid of disabilities on the ground of religion. It is only beginning to treat any *men* as citizens, except the rich and a favoured portion of the middle class. Can we wonder that it has not yet done as much for women?" ("Enfranchisement of Women," Mrs. Mill. In J. S. Mill's "Discussions and Dissertations," Vol. II., page 421.) The difference between men and women in all civil rights is, however, with few, although important, exceptions, confined to married women; *i.e.*, women in relation with men. Unmarried women of all ages suffer under comparatively few disabilities; it is marriage which brings with it the weight of injustice and of legal degradation.

In savage times marriage was a matter either of force, fraud, or purchase. Women were merchandise, by the sale of whom their male relatives profited, or they were captives in war, the spoil of the conqueror, or they were stolen away from the paternal home. In all cases, however, the possession once obtained, they became the property of the men who married them, and the husband was their "lord," their "master." In the old Hebrew books—still accounted sacred by Jews and Christians—the wife is regarded as the property of her husband. A man may "sell his daughter to be a maidservant;" *i.e.*, a concubine, as is shown by the following verse (Ex. xxi. 7), and Jacob served seven years for each of his wives, Leah and Rachel; his other two wives were his by gift, and were rather concubines than recognised wives, their children counting to their mistresses. If a Hebrew conquered his enemies, and saw "among the captives a beautiful woman, and hast a desire unto her, that thou wouldst have her to thy wife," he might take her home, and become her husband, "and she shall be thy wife" (Deut. xxi. 10-14). After the destruction of Benjamin, as related in Judges xx., it was arranged that the survivors should possess themselves of women as wives by force and fraud: "Lie in wait in the vineyards, and see and behold if the daughters of Shiloh come out to dance in dances, then come ye out of the vineyards, and catch you every man his wife...... And the children of Benjamin did so, and took their wives according to their number, of them that danced, whom they caught" (Judges xxi. 20, 21, 23). The same plan was adopted by the Romans in their earliest days, when they needed wives. Romulus invited the people of the Sabines and the neighbouring towns to see some public games, and in the midst of the show the Romans rushed in and carried off all the marriageable maidens they could lay hands on (Liddell's "History of Rome," p. 20). These instances may be objected to as legendary, but they are faithful pictures of the rough wooing of early times. Among some barbarous nations the winning of a bride is still harsher: the bridegroom rushes into the father's house knocks the maiden down, picks up her senseless body, flings it over his shoulder, and runs for his life; he is pursued by the youth of the village, pelted with stones, sticks, &c., and has to win his wife by sheer strength and swiftness. In some tribes this is a mere marriage ceremony, a survival from the time when the fight was a real one, and amongst ourselves the slipper thrown after the departing bridegroom and bride is a direct descendant of the heavier missiles thrown with deadly intent thousands of years ago by our remote ancestors. Amongst many semi-barbarous nations the wives are still bought; in some parts of Africa the wooer pays a certain number of cows for his bride; in other places, money or goods are given in exchange. The point to be noted is that the wife is literally taken by force, or bought; she is not free to choose her husband; she does not give herself to him; she is a piece of property, handed over by her original owner—her father—to her new owner—her husband—in exchange for certain solid money or money's worth; hence she becomes the property of the man who has paid for her.

In an admirable article in the *Westminster Review* for April, 1876, the following striking passage is to be found:

"As Aristotle long since remarked, among savages women and slaves hold the same rank. Women are bought primarily as slaves, to drudge and toil for their masters, whilst their function as wives is secondary and subordinate. It is more right to say of polygamous people that their slaves are also their wives, than to say that their wives are slaves. They are purchased as slaves, they work as slaves, and they live as slaves. 'The history of uncultivated nations,' it has been said, 'uniformly represents the women as in a state of abject slavery, from which they slowly emerge as civilisation advances.' In Canada a strap, a kettle, and a faggot are placed in the new bride's cabin, to indicate that it will be henceforth her duty to carry burdens, dress food, and procure wood for her husband. In Circassia it is the women who till and manure the ground, and in parts of China they follow the plough. A Moorish wife digs and sows and reaps the corn, and an Arabian wife feeds and cleans and saddles her master's horse. Indeed, the sole business of Bedouin wives is to cook and work, and perform all the menial offices connected with tent-life. . . . From the absolute power of a savage over his slaves flow all those rights over a woman from which the marital rights of our own time are the genealogical descendants. . . . A trace of it [purchase] is found in the following customs of old English law:—'The woman at the church-door was given of her father, or some other man of the next of her kin, into the hands of her husband, and he laid down gold and silver for her upon the book, as though he did buy her.'" This custom is still maintained in the Church ritual; the priest asks: "Who giveth this woman to be married to this man?" and when the man gives the ring to the priest, he gives money with it, receiving back the ring to give the woman, but the money remaining, a survival of the time when wives were literally bought.

By the old Roman laws, the married woman had no personal rights; she was but the head slave in her husband's house, absolutely subject in all things to her lord. As the Romans became civilised, these disabilities were gradually removed. It is important to remember these facts, as these are the origin of our own marriage laws, and our common law really grows out of them.

One other point must be noticed, before dealing immediately with the English marriage laws, and that is the influence exerted over them by ecclesiastical Christianity

The Old Testament expressly sanctions polygamy; but while the New Testament does not proscribe it—except in the case of bishops and deacons—ecclesiastical Christianity has generally been in favour of monogamy; at the same time, both the New Testament and the Church have insisted on the inferiority of the female sex; "the husband is the head of the wife" (Eph. v. 23); "wives, submit yourselves unto your own husbands" (Col. iii. 18); "your women . . . are commanded to be under obedience" (1 Cor. xiv. 34); "ye wives, be in subjection to your own husbands . . . even as Sara obeyed Abraham, calling him lord, whose daughters ye are as long as ye do well" (1 Pet. iii. 1, 6). The common law of England is quite in accordance with this ancient Eastern teaching, and regards men as superior to women; "Among the children of the purchaser, males take before females, or, as our male lawgivers have expressed it, the worthiest of blood shall be preferred" ("Comm. on the Laws of England," J. Stephen, 7th ed. vol. i. p. 402).

The feudal system did much, of course, to perpetuate the subjection of women, it being to the interest of the lord paramount that the fiefs should descend in the male line: in those rough ages, when wars and civil feuds were almost perpetual, it was inevitable that the sex with the biggest body and strongest sinews should have the upper hand; the pity is that English gentlemen to-day are content to allow the law to remain unaltered, when the whole face of society has changed.

Let us now turn to the disabilities imposed upon women by marriage.

Blackstone lays down, in his world-famous "Commentaries on the Laws of England," that the first of the "absolute rights of every Englishman" is "the legal and uninterrupted enjoyment of his life, his limbs, his body, his health, and his reputation" (9th ed., bk. 1, p. 129). The second right is personal liberty, and he says: "the confinement of a person in anywise is an imprisonment. So that the keeping a man against his will in a private house. . . . is an imprisonment" (Ibid, 136). The third is property, "which consists in the free use and enjoyment of all his acquisitions, without any control or diminution, save only by the laws of the land" (Ibid, 138). A subordinate right, necessary for the enforcement of the others, is "that of applying to the courts of justice for redress of injuries." I shall proceed to show that a married woman is deprived of these rights by the mere fact of her marriage.

In the first place, by marriage a woman loses her legal existence; the law does not recognize her, excepting in some few cases, when it becomes conscious of her existence in order to punish her for some crime or misdemeanour. Blackstone says—and no subsequent legislation has in any way modified his dictum: "By marriage the husband and wife are one person in law; that is, the very being or legal existence of the woman is suspended during the marriage, or at least is incorporated or consolidated into that of the husband; under whose wing, protection, and *cover*, she performs every thing; and is therefore called in our law-French a *feme covert*" (p. 442). "Husband and wife are one person in law" (Comyn's Digest, 5th ed., vol. ii., p. 208), and from this it follows that "by no conveyance at the common law could the husband give an estate to his wife;" that "a husband cannot covenant or contract with his wife," even for her own advantage, and that any prenuptial contract made with her as to money she shall enjoy for her separate use after marriage, becomes void as soon as she is married. All covenants for the wife's benefit must be made with some one else, and the husband must covenant with some other man or unmarried woman who acts as trustee for the wife. This is the fundamental wrong from which all the others flow: "'Husband and wife are one person,' and that one is the husband." The wife's body, her reputation, are no longer her own. She can gain no legal redress for injury, for the law does not recognize her existence except under cover of her husband's suit. In some cases more modern legislation has so far become conscious of her, as to protect her against her husband, and if this protection separates her from him, it leaves her the more utterly at the mercy of the world.

Various curious results flow, in criminal law, from this supposition that husband and wife are only one person. They are incompetent—except in a few special instances—to give evidence for or against each other in criminal cases; if a woman's husband be one of several defendants indicted together, the woman cannot give evidence either for or against any of them. Where the wife of an accomplice is the only person to confirm her husband's statement, the statement falls to the ground, as, in practice, confirmation thereof is required; in the case of Rex *v.* Neal (7 C. and P.

168), Justice Park said: "Confirmation by the wife is, in this case, really no confirmation at all. The wife and the accomplice must be taken as one for this purpose. The prisoners must be acquitted." They may, however, be severally called as witnesses by the prosecution and the defence, in order that they may contradict each other. Where the wife has suffered personal violence from her husband she is permitted to swear the peace against him, and in divorce suits husband and wife are both admissible as witnesses. A wife who sets fire to her husband's house may escape punishment, as in the case of Rex. *v.* March: "March and his wife had lived separate for about two years; and, previous to the act, when she applied for the candle with which it was done, she said it was to set her husband's house on fire, because she wanted to burn him to death. Upon a case reserved upon the question whether it was an offence within the 7 and 8 George IV., cap. 30, sec. 2, for a wife to set fire to her husband's house for the purpose of doing him a personal injury, the conviction was held wrong, the learned judges thinking that to constitute the offence, it was essential that there should be an intent to injure or defraud some third person, not one identified with herself" (Ibid, p. 899). Identification with one's beloved may be delightful in theory, but when, in practice, it comes to being burned at pleasure, surely the greatest stickler for the "twain being one" must feel some twinges of doubt. The identity of husband and wife is often by no means advantageous to the husband, for he thereby becomes responsible, to a great extent, for his wife's misdoings. "For slanderous words spoken by the wife, libel published by her alone, trespass, assault and battery, &c., he is liable to be so sued, whether the act was committed with or without his sanction or knowledge. . . . . And wherever the action is grounded on a tort, committed by the wife, it no way affects the necessity of joining the husband, that the parties are living apart, nor even that they are divorced *a mensâ et thoro*, or that the wife is living in adultery" (Lush's "Common Law Practice," 2nd ed., p. 156). Pleasant position for a man whose wife may have left him, to be suddenly dragged before a court of justice for some misdeed of hers, of which he may never have heard until he finds himself summoned to answer for it! A large amount of injustice arises from this absurd fiction that two are one; it sometimes injures, sometimes protects the married woman, and it often shields those who have wronged her; but whether it injure or whether it protect, it is equally vicious; it is *unjust*, and injustice is a radical injury to a community, and by destroying the reasonableness and the certainty of the law, it saps that reverence for it which is one of the safeguards of society.

Let us now take Blackstone's "rights of every Englishman," and see what rights the common law allowed to a married Englishwoman. A married woman is not protected by the law in the "uninterrupted enjoyment of" her "limbs," her "body," or her "reputation." On the contrary: "If a wife be injured in her person, or her property, she can bring no action for redress without her husband's concurrence, and in his name as well as her own" (Blackstone, p. 443). If in a railway accident a married woman has her leg broken, she cannot sue the railway company for damages; she is not a damaged *person*; in the eye of the law, she is a piece of damaged *property*, and the compensation is to be made to her owner. If she is attacked and beaten she cannot summon her assailant; her master suffers loss and inconvenience by the assault on his housekeeper, and his action is necessary to obtain redress. If she is libelled, she cannot protect her good name, for she is incapable by herself of maintaining an action. In fact, it is not even needful that her name should appear at all in the matter: "the husband may sue alone for loss of his wife's society by injury done to her, or for damage to her reputation" (Comyn's Digest, under "Baron and Feme"). The following curious statement of the law on this head is given in Broom's "Commentaries:" "Injuries which may be offered to a person, considered as a husband, and which are cognizable in a court of common law, are principally three: 1, abduction, or taking away a man's wife; 2, beating her; 3, indirectly causing her some personal hurt, by negligence or otherwise. 1. As to the first sort, abduction, or taking her away, this may either be by fraud and persuasion, or open violence; though the law in both cases supposes force and constraint, the wife having no power to consent, and therefore gives a remedy by action of trespass; and the husband is also entitled to recover damages in an action on the case against such as persuade and entice the wife to live separate from him without a sufficient cause. . . . 2, 3. The second and third injuries above mentioned are constituted by beating a man's wife, or otherwise ill-using her; or causing hurt to her by negligence. For a common assault upon, or battery, or imprisonment, of the wife, the law gives the usual remedy to recover damages, by action of trespass, which must be brought in the names of the husband and wife jointly: but if the beating or other maltreatment be so enormous, that thereby the husband is deprived for any time of the company and assistance of his wife, the law then gives him a separate remedy by action for this ill-usage, *per quod consortium amisit*, in which he may recover a satisfaction in damages. By a provision of the C. L. Proc. Act, 1852, s. 40, in an action by husband and wife jointly for an injury to the wife, the husband is now allowed to add a claim in his own right—as for the loss of the wife's society—or where a joint trespass and assault have been committed on the husband and his wife" (vol. iii., pp. 149, 150). So far is recognised the husband's complete claim over his wife's person, that anyone who receives a married woman into his house and gives her shelter there after having received notice from her husband that he is not to permit her to remain under his roof, actually becomes liable in damages to the husband. The husband cannot sue for damages if he has turned his wife out of doors, or if he has lost his right of control by cruelty or adultery; short of this, he may obtain damages against any friend or relative of the woman who gives her shelter. The wife has no such remedy against anyone who may induce the husband to live apart, or who may give him houseroom at his own wish. The reason for the law being as we find it, is stated by Broom without the smallest compunction: "We may observe that in these relative injuries notice is only taken of the wrong done to the superior of the parties related, by the breach and dissolution of either the relation itself, or at least the advantage accruing therefrom: while the loss of the inferior by such injuries is, except where the death of a parent has been caused by negligence, unregarded. One reason for which may be, that the inferior has no kind of property in the company, care, or assistance of the superior, as the superior is held to have in that of the inferior; and therefore the inferior can, in contemplation of law, suffer no loss consequential on a wrongful act done to his superior. The wife cannot recover damages for the beating of her husband. The child has no property in his father or guardian. And the servant, whose master is disabled, does not thereby lose his maintenance or wages" (Ibid, p. 153). A man may recover damages equally for the injury done to his servant or to his wife; in both cases he loses their services, and the law recompenses him. A peculiarly disgusting phase of this claim is where a husband claims damages against a co-respondent in the divorce court; if a wife be unfaithful, the husband can not only get a divorce, but can also claim a money payment from the seducer to make up for the damage he has sustained by losing his wife's services. An unmarried girl, under age, is regarded as the property of her father, and the father may bring an action against her seducer for the loss of his daughter's services. It is not the woman who is injured, or who has any redress; it is her male owner who can recover damages for the injury done to his property.

If a wife be separated from her husband, either by deed or by judicial decree, she has no remedy for injury or for libel, unless by the doubtful plan of using her husband's name without his consent. On this injustice Lord Lyndhurst, speaking in the House of Lords in 1856, said: "A wife is separated from her husband by a decree of the Ecclesiastical Court, the reason for that decree being the husband's misconduct—his cruelty, it may be, or his adultery. From that moment the wife is almost in a state of outlawry. She may not enter into a contract, or if she do, she has no means of enforcing it. The law, so far from protecting, oppresses her. She is homeless, helpless, hopeless, and almost wholly destitute of civil rights. She is liable to all manner of injustice, whether by plot or by violence. She may be wronged in all possible ways, and her character may be mercilessly defamed; yet she has no redress. She is at the mercy of her enemies. Is that fair? Is that honest? Can it be vindicated upon any principle of justice, of mercy or of common humanity?"

A married woman loses control over her own body; it belongs to her owner, not to herself; no force, no violence, on the husband's part in conjugal relations is regarded as possible by the law; she may be suffering, ill, it matters not; force or constraint is recognised by the law as rape, in all cases save that of marriage; the law "holds it to be felony to force even a concubine or harlot" (Broom's "Commentaries," vol. iv., p. 255), but no rape can be committed by a husband on a wife; the consent given in marriage is held to cover the life, and if—as sometimes occurs—a miscarriage or premature confinement be brought on by the husband's selfish passions, no offence is committed in the eye of the law, for the wife is the husband's property, and by marriage she has lost the right of control over her own body. The English marriage law sweeps away all the tenderness, all the grace, all the generosity of love, and transforms conjugal affection into a hard and brutal legal right.

By the common law the husband has a right to inflict corporal punishment on his wife, and although this right is now much restricted, the effect of the law is seen in the brutal treatment of wives among the rougher classes, and the light—sometimes no—punishment inflicted on wife-beaters. The common law is thus given by Blackstone: "The husband also (by the old law) might give his wife moderate correction. For as he is to answer for her misbehaviour, the law thought it reasonable to entrust him with this power of restraining her, by domestic chastisement, in the same moderation that a man is allowed to correct his apprentices or children. The lower rank of people, who were always fond of the old common law, still claim and exert their ancient privilege." Blackstone grimly adds, after saying this is all for woman's protection: "So great a favourite is the female sex of the laws of England" (444 and 445). This "ancient privilege" is very commonly exercised at the present time. A man who dragged his wife out of bed (1877), and, pulling off her nightdress, roasted her in front of the fire, was punished (?) by being bound over to keep the peace for a short period. Men who knock their wives down, who dance on them, who drag them about by the hair, &c., are condemned to brief terms of imprisonment, and are then allowed to resume their marital authority, and commence a new course of ill-treatment. In dealing later with the changes I shall recommend in the marriage laws, this point will come under discussion.

Coming to the second "right," of "personal liberty," we find that a married woman has no such right. Blackstone says, as we have seen: "the confinement of a person in any wise is an imprisonment. So that the keeping a man against his will in a private house . . . is an imprisonment" (p. 136). But a husband may legally act as his wife's gaoler; "the courts of law will still permit a husband to restrain his wife of her liberty, in case of any gross misbehaviour" (Blackstone, p. 445). "If the wife squanders his estate, or goes into lewd company, he may deprive her of liberty" (Comyn's Digest, under "Baron and Feme"). Broom says that at the present time "there can be no question respecting the common-law right of a husband to restrain his wife of her personal liberty, with a view to prevent her going into society of which he disapproves, or otherwise disobeying his rightful authority; such right must not, however, be exercised unnecessarily, or with undue severity: and the moment that the wife by returning to her conjugal duties, makes restraint of her person unnecessary, such restraint becomes unlawful" (vol. i, p. 547). Last year (1877) a publican at Spilsby chained up his wife to the wall from one day to the afternoon of the following one, in order, he said, to keep her from drink; the magistrates dismissed him without punishment. It may be argued that a woman should not get drunk, go into bad company, &c. Quite so; neither should a man. But would men admit, that under similar circumstances, a wife should have legal power to deprive her husband of liberty? If not, there is no reason in justice why the husband should be permitted to exercise it. Offences known to the law should be punished by the law, and by the law alone; offences which the law cannot touch should entail no punishment on an adult at the hands of a private individual. Public disapproval may brand them, but no personal chastisement should be inflicted by arbitrary and irresponsible power.

The third right, of "property," has also no existence for married women. Unmarried women have here no ground for complaint: "A *feme sole*, before her marriage, may do all acts for disposition, etc., of her lands or goods which any man in the same circumstances may do" (Comyn's Digest, under "Baron and Feme"). The disabilities which affect women as women do not touch property; a *feme sole* may own real or personal estate, buy, sell, give, contract, sue, and be sued, just as though she were of the "worthier blood;" it is marriage that, like felony and insanity, destroys her capability as proprietor. According to the common law—with which we will deal first—the following results accrued from marriage:—

"Whatever personal property belonged to the wife before marriage, is by marriage absolutely vested in the husband. . . . in chattel interests, the sole and absolute property vests in the husband, to be disposed of at his pleasure, if he chooses to take possession of them" (Blackstone, book ii. 443). If he takes possession, they do not, at his death, revert to the wife, but go to his heirs or to anyone he chooses by will. "If a woman be seized of an estate of inheritance, and marries, her husband shall be seized of in her right" (Comyn's Digest, under "Baron and Feme"). If a woman own land in her own right, all rents and profits are not hers, but her husband's; even arrears of rents due before coverture become his; he may make a lease of her land, commencing after his own death, and she is barred, although she survive him; he may dispose of his wife's interest; it may be forfeited by his crime, seized for his debt; she only regains it if she survives him and he has not disposed of it. If a woman, before marriage, lets her land on a lease, the rental, after marriage, becomes her husband's, and her receipt is not a good discharge. If a wife grants a rent-charge out of her own lands (or, rather, what should be her own) without the husband's consent, it is void. All personal goods that "the wife has in possession in her own right, are vested in her husband by the marriage" (Ibid); gifts to her become his; if he sues for a debt due to his wife, and recovers it, it is his; if a legacy be left her, it goes to him; after his death, all that was her personal property originally, goes to his executors and administrators, and does not revert to her; so absolutely is all she may become possessed of his by law that if, after a divorce *a mensâ et thoro*, the wife should sue another woman for adultery with her husband, and should be awarded her costs, the husband can release the woman from payment.

If a woman own land and lease it, then if, during marriage, the husband reduce it into possession, "as where rent accruing on a lease granted by the wife *dum sola* is received by a person appointed for that purpose during the husband's life," under such circumstances the husband's "executors, not his widow, must sue the agent" (Lush's "Common Law Practice," 2nd. ed., p. 27). In a case where "certain leasehold property was conveyed to trustees upon trust to permit the wife to receive the rents thereof to her sole and separate use, and she after marriage deposited with her trustees part of such rents and died; it was held that her husband might recover the same in an action in his own right. Such money, so deposited, was not a *chose in action* belonging to the wife, but money belonging to the husband, the trust having been discharged in the payment of the rents to the wife" (Ibid, p. 97). Marriage, to a man, is regarded as a kind of lucrative business: "The next method of acquiring property in goods and chattels is by marriage; whereby those chattels, which belonged formerly to the wife, are by act of law vested in the husband, with the same degree of property, and with the same powers, as the wife, when sole, had over them . . . A distinction is taken between chattels real and chattels personal, and of chattels personal, whether in possession or reversion, or in action. A chattel real vests in the husband, not absolutely, but *sub modo*. As, in case of a lease for years, the husband shall receive all the rents and profits of it, and may, if he pleases, sell, surrender, or dispose of it during the coverture; if he be outlawed or attainted, it shall be forfeited to the king; it is liable to execution for his debts; and if he survives his wife, it is to all intents and purposes his own. Yet, if he has made no disposition thereof in his lifetime, and dies before his wife, he cannot dispose of it by will: for, the husband having made no alteration in the property during his life, it never was transferred from the wife; but after his death she shall remain in her ancient possession, and it shall not go to his executors. If, however, the wife die in the husband's lifetime, the chattel real survives to him. As to chattels personal (or choses) in action, as debts upon bonds, contracts, and the like, these the husband may have if he pleases; that is, if he reduces them into possession by receiving or recovering them at law. And upon such receipt or recovery they are absolutely and entirely his own; and shall go to his executors or administrators, or as he shall bequeath them by will, and shall not revest in the wife. But, if he dies before he has recovered or reduced them into possession, so that, at his death, they still continue choses in action, they shall survive to the wife; for the husband never exerted the power he had of obtaining an exclusive property in them. If the wife die before the husband has reduced choses in action into possession, he does not become entitled by survivorship; nevertheless, he may, by becoming her administrator, gain a title. Chattels in possession, such as ready money and the like, vest absolutely in the husband, and he may deal with them, either whilst living, or by his will, as he pleases. Where the interest of the wife is reversionary, the husband's power is but small; unless it falls into possession during the marriage, his contracts or engagements do not bind it" ("Comm. on the Laws of England," Broom and Hadley, vol. ii., pp. 618, 619). So highly does the law value the claims of a husband that it recognizes them as existing even before marriage; for if a woman who has contracted an engagement to marry dispose of her property privately, settle it on herself, or on her children, without the cognizance of the man to whom she is engaged, such settlement or disposition may be set aside by the husband as a fraud.

So cruel, as regards property, was felt to be the action of the common law, that the wealthy devised means to escape from it, and women of property were protected on their marriage by "marriage settlements," whereby they were contracted out of the law. A woman's property was by this means, "settled on herself;" it was necessary to treat her as incapable, so her property was not in her own power but was vested in trustees for her separate use; thus the principal, or the estate, was protected, but the whole interest or rental, as before, could be taken by the husband the moment it was received by the wife; her signature became necessary to draw it, but the moment it came into her possession it ceased to be hers. The next step was an attempt to protect women's money in their own hands; terrible cases of wrong were continually arising: men who deserted their wives, and left them to maintain the burden of a family, came back after the wife had accumulated a little property, sold the furniture, pocketed the proceeds, and departed, leaving the wife to recommence her labours. Orders of protection were given by magistrates, but these were not found sufficient. At last, parliamentary interference was called for with an urgency that could no longer be resisted, and a Bill to amend the laws relating to married women's property was introduced into the House of Commons. How sore was the need of such amendment may be seen from the following extracts :—

Mr. Russell Gurney, in moving (April 14, 1869) the second reading of the Bill, observed: "It is now proposed that, for the first time in our history, the property of one half of the married people of this country should receive the protection of the law. Up to this time the property of a wife has had no protection from the law, or rather, he should say, in the eye of the law it has had no existence. From the moment of her marriage the wife, in fact, possesses no property; whatever she may up to that time have possessed, by the very act of marriage passes from her, and any gift or bequest made to her becomes at once the property of the husband. Nay, even that which one might suppose to be her inalienable right, the fruit of her mental or bodily toil, is denied her. She may be gifted with powers which enable her to earn an ample fortune, but the moment it is earned, it is not hers, it is her husband's. In fact, from the time of her entering into what is described as an honourable estate, the law pronounces her unfit to hold any property whatever."

Mr. Jessel (now Master of the Rolls) in seconding the motion, in the course of an able and impassioned speech, said: "The existing law is a relic of slavery, and the House is now asked to abolish the last remains of slavery in England. In considering what ought to be the nature of the law, we cannot deny that no one should be deprived of the power of disposition, unless on proof of unfitness to exercise that power; and it is not intelligible on what principle a woman should be considered incapable of contracting immediately after she has, with the sanction of the law, entered into the most important contract conceivable. The slavery laws of antiquity are the origin of the common law on this subject. The Roman law originally regarded the position of a wife as similar to that of a daughter who had no property, and might be sold into slavery at the will of her father. When the Roman law became that of a civilised people, the position of the wife was altogether changed. . . . The ancient Germans—from whom our law is derived—put the woman into the power of her husband in the same sense as the ancient Roman law did. She became his slave. The law of slavery—whether Roman or English—for we once had slaves and slave-laws in England—gave to the master of a slave the two important rights of flogging and imprisoning him. A slave could not possess property of his own, and could not make contracts except for his master's benefit, and the master alone could sue for an injury to the slave; while the only liability of the master was that he must not let his slave starve. This is exactly the position of the wife under the English law; the husband has the right of flogging and imprisoning her, as may be seen by those who read Blackstone's chapter on the relations of husband and wife. She cannot possess property—she cannot contract, except it is as his agent; and he alone can sue if she is libelled or suffers a personal injury; while all the husband is compellable to do for her is to pay for necessaries. It is astonishing that a law founded on such principles should have survived to the nineteenth century."

A quotation from a later debate finds its fit place here: Mr. Hinde Palmer, in moving (February 19, 1873) the second reading of the Married Woman's Property Act

(1870) Amendment Bill, pointed out that the common law was, that by marriage "the whole of a woman's personal property was immediately vested in her husband, and placed entirely at his disposal. By contracting marriage, a woman forfeited all her property. In 1868, the Chancellor of the Exchequer, Mr. Lowe, said: 'Show me what crime there is in matrimony that it should be visited by the same punishment as high treason—namely, confiscation, for that is really the fact.' Mr. Mill, too, speaking on that question, said that a large portion of the inhabitants of this country were in the anomalous position of having imposed on them, without having done anything to deserve it, what we inflicted on the worst criminals as a penalty: like felons, they were incapable of holding property."

Some great and beneficial changes were made by the Acts of 1870 and 1873, although much yet remains to be done. By the Act of 1870, the wages and earnings of married women were protected; they were made capable of depositing money in the savings' banks in their own names; they might hold property in the Funds in their own names, and have the dividends paid to them; they might hold fully-paid up shares, or stock, to which no liability was attached; property in societies might be retained by them; money coming to a married woman as the next-of-kin, or one of the next-of-kin to an intestate, or by deed or will, was made her own, provided that such money did not exceed £200; the rents and profits of freehold, copyhold, or customary-hold property inherited by a married woman were to be her own; a married woman might insure her own or her husband's life; might, under some circumstances, maintain an action in her own name; married women were made liable for the maintenance of their husbands and children. The Act of 1873 relates entirely to the recovery of debts contracted by the woman before marriage. It will be perceived that these Acts are very inadequate as regards placing married women in a just position towards their property, but they are certainly a step in the right direction. The Acts only apply to those women who have been married subsequently to their passing.

One great omission in them will have to be promptly remedied, both for the sake of married women and for the sake of their creditors: while a married woman now may, under some circumstances, sue, no machinery is provided whereby she may be sued—without joining her husband.

In an admirable letter to the *Times* of March 14, 1878, Mrs. Ursule Bright, alluding to the "obscurity and uncertainty of the law," points out

"The effect of that obscurity upon the credit of respectable married women earning their own and their children's bread, in any employment or business carried on separately from their husband; the inconvenience and risk to their creditors is, as you have most ably pointed out, great; but the injury to honest wives is far greater. It puts them at a considerable disadvantage in the labour market and in business. A married woman, for instance, keeping a little shop, may sue for debts due to her, but has no corresponding liability to be sued. If the whereabouts of the husband is not very clearly defined, it is evident she may have some difficulty in obtaining credit.

"Again, what employer of labour can with any security engage the services of a married woman? She may leave her work at the mill at an hour's notice unfinished, and her employer has no remedy against her for breach of contract, as a married woman can make no contract which is legally binding. There is no question that such a state of the law must operate as a restriction upon her power to support herself and family.

"The state of muddle of the present law is almost inconceivable. Even now a woman need not pay her debts contracted before marriage out of earnings made after marriage. Suppose an artist or a literary woman to marry when burdened with debts and having no property; should she be earning £1,000 or £10,000 a year by her profession after marriage, these earnings could not be made liable for her debts contracted before marriage."

It cannot too plainly be repeated that non-liability to be sued means non-existence of credit.

The law, as it stands at present, is the old Common Law, modified by the Acts of 1870 and 1873. Archbold says—dealing with indictments for theft—"Where the person named as owner appears to be a married woman, the defendant must, unless the indictment is amended, be acquitted . . . because in law the goods are the property of the husband; even though she be living apart from her husband upon an income arising from property vested in trustees for her separate use, because the goods cannot be the property of the trustees; and, in law, a married woman has no property" (Archbold's "Criminal Cases," p. 43). Archbold gives as exceptions to this general rule, where a judicial separation has taken place, where the wife has obtained a protection order, or where the property is such as is covered by the Married Women's Property Act, 1870. "Where a married woman lived apart from her husband, upon an income arising from property vested in trustees for her separate use, the judges held that a house which she lived in was properly described as her husband's dwelling-house, though she paid the rent out of her separate property, and the husband had never been in it. R. *v.* French, R. *v.* R., 491" (Ibid, p. 521). If a burglary be committed in a house belonging to a married woman, the house must be said to be the dwelling-house of her husband, or the burglar will be acquitted; if she be living separate from her husband, paying her own rent out of money secured for her separate use, it makes no difference; it was decided, in the case of Rex *v.* French, that a married woman could own no property, and that the house must, therefore, belong to the husband. If a married woman picks up a purse in the road and is robbed of it, the property vests in the husband: "Where goods are in the possession of the wife, they must be laid as the goods of her husband; thus, if A is indicted for stealing the goods of B, and it appears that B was a *feme covert* at the time, A must be acquitted. And even if the wife have only received money as the agent of another person, and she is robbed of that money before her husband receives it into his possession, still it is well laid as his money in an indictment for larceny. An indictment charging the stealing of a £5 Bank of England note, the property of E. Wall, averring, in the usual way, that the money secured by the note was due and payable to E. Wall; it appeared that E. Wall's wife had been employed to sell sheep belonging to her father, of or in which her husband never had either possession or any interest, and she received the note in payment for the sheep, and it was stolen from her before she left the place where she received it. It was objected that the note never was the property of E. Wall, either actually or constructively; the money secured by it was not his, and he had no qualified property in it, as it never was in his possession; but it was held that the property was properly laid" (Russell on Crimes, 5th ed., vol. ii., pp. 243, 244). Yet even a child, in the eye of the law, has property, and if his clothes are stolen, it is safer to allege them to be the child's property. The main principle of English law remains unaltered by recent legislation, that "a married woman has no property." Married women share incapacity to manage property with minors and lunatics; minors, lunatics, and married women are taken care of by trustees; minors become of age, lunatics often recover, married women remain incapable during the whole of their married life.

Being incapable of holding property, a married woman is, of course, incapable of making a will. Here, also, the Common Law may be checkmated. She may make a will "by virtue of a power reserved to her, or of a marriage settlement, or with her husband's assent, or it may be made by her to carry her separate estate; and the court in determining whether or not such will is entitled to probate, will not go minutely into the question, but will only require that the testatrix had a power reserved to her, or was entitled to separate estate, and will, if so satisfied, grant probate to her executor, leaving it to the Court of Chancery, as the court of construction, to say what portion of her estate, if any, will pass under such will. In this case the husband, though he may not be entitled to take probate of his wife's will, may administer to such of her effects as do not pass under the will" ("Comm. on the Laws of England," Broom and Hadley, vol. iii., pp. 427, 428). Thus we see that a husband may will away from his wife her own original property, but a wife may not even will away her own, unless the right be specially reserved to her before marriage. And yet it is urged that women have no need of votes, their interests being so well looked after by their fathers, husbands, and brothers!

We have thus seen that the "rights of every Englishman" are destroyed in women by marriage; one would imagine that matrimony was a crime for which a woman deserved punishment, and that confiscation and outlawry were the fit rewards of her misdeed.

From these three great fundamental wrongs flow a large number of legal disabilities. Take the case of a prisoner accused of misdemeanour; he is often set free on his own recognizances; but a married woman cannot be so released, for she is incapable of becoming bail or of giving her own recognizances; she is here again placed in bad company: "no person who has been convicted of any crime by which he has become infamous is allowed to be surety for any person charged or suspected of an indictable offence. Nor can a married woman, or an infant, or a prisoner in custody, be bail" (Archbold, p. 88). Let us now suppose that a woman be accused of some misdemeanour, and be committed for trial: she desires to have her case tried by a higher court than the usual one, and wishes to remove the indictment by writ of *certiorari:* she finds that the advantage is denied her, because, as a married woman, she has no property, and she cannot therefore enter into the necessary recognizances to pay costs in the case of a conviction. Thus a married woman finds herself placed at a cruel disadvantage as compared with an unmarried woman or with men.

In matters of business, difficulties arise on every hand: a married woman is incapable of making a contract; if she takes a house without her husband's knowledge and without stating that she is married, the landlord may repudiate the contract; if she states that she is married, the landlord knows that she is unable to make a legal contract, and refuses to let or lease to her, without heavy security. If she buys things, she cannot be sued for non-payment without making the husband a defendant, and she consequently finds that she has no credit. If she is cheated, she cannot sue, except in cases covered by the recent Acts, without joining her husband, and so she has often to submit to be wronged. "A *feme covert* cannot sue without her husband being joined as co-plaintiff, so long as the relation of marriage subsists. It matters not that he is an alien, and has left the country; or that, being a subject, he has absconded from the realm as a bankrupt or for other purpose; or that he has become permanently resident abroad; or that they are living apart under a deed of separation; or have been divorced *a mensâ et thoro;* for none of these events dissolve or work a suspension of the marriage contract, and so long as that endures, the wife is unable to sue alone, whatever the cause of action may be. This disability results from the rule of law which vests in the husband not only all the goods and chattels which belonged to the wife at the time of the marriage, but also all which she acquires afterwards" (Lush's "Common Law Practice," 2nd ed., pp. 33, 34). The same principle governs all suits against a married woman; the husband must be sued with her: "In all actions brought against a *feme covert* while the relation of marriage subsists, the husband must be joined for conformity, it being an inflexible rule of law that a wife shall not be sued without her husband. . . . If therefore a wife enters into a bond jointly with her husband, or makes a bill of exchange, promissory note, or any other contract, she cannot be sued thereon, but the action should be brought against, and the bond, bill, &c., alleged to have been made by, the husband" (Ibid, p. 75).

The thoughtful author of the "Rights of Women" remarks that the incapacity to sue is "traceable to the time when disputes were settled by the judgment of arms. A man represents his wife at law now, because in the days of the judicial combat he was her champion-at-arms, and she is unable to sue now, because she was unable to fight then" (p. 22). The explanation is a very reasonable one, and is only an additional proof of the need of alteration in the law; our marriage laws are, as has been shown above, the survival of barbarism, and we only ask that modern civilisation will alter and improve them as it does everything else: trial by combat has been destroyed; ought not its remains to be buried out of sight? The consequence of these business disabilities is that a married woman finds herself thwarted at every turn, and if she be trying to gain a livelihood, and be separated from her husband, she is constantly pained and annoyed by the marriage-fetter, which hinders her activity and checks her efforts to make her way. The notion that irresponsibility is an advantage is an entirely mistaken one; an irresponsible person cannot be dealt with in business matters, and is shut out of all the usual independent ways of obtaining a livelihood. Authorship and servitude are the only paths really open to married women; in every other career they find humiliating obstacles which it needs both courage and perseverance to surmount.

Married women rank among the "persons in subjection to the power of others;" they thus come among those who in many cases are not criminally liable; "infants under the age of discretion," persons who are *non compotes mentis* (not of sound mind), and persons acting under coercion, are not criminally liable for their misdeeds. A married woman is presumed to act under her husband's coercion, unless the contrary be proved, and she may thus escape punishment for her wrongdoings: "Constraint of a superior is sometimes allowed as an excuse for criminal misconduct, by reason of the matrimonial subjection of the wife to her husband; but neither a son, nor a servant is excused for the commission of any crime by the command or coercion of the parent or master. Thus, if a woman commit theft, or burglary, by the coercion of her husband, or even in his company, which the law *primâ facie* construes a coercion, she is dispunishable, being considered to have acted by compulsion, and not of her own will" ("Comm. on the Laws of England," Broom and Hadley, vol. iv., p. 27). "A *feme covert* is so much favoured in respect of that power and authority which her husband has over her, that she shall not suffer any punishment for committing a bare theft, or even a burglary, by the coercion of her husband, or in his company, which the law construes a coercion" (Russell "On Crimes," vol. i., p. 139). "Where the wife is to be considered merely as the servant of the husband, she will not be answerable for the consequences of his breach of duty, however fatal, though she may be privy to his conduct. C. Squire and his wife were indicted for the murder of a boy;" he had been cruelly treated by both, and died "from debility and want of proper food and nourishment;" "Lawrence, J., directed the jury, that as the wife was the servant of the husband, it was not her duty to provide the apprentice with sufficient food and nourishment, and that she was not guilty of any breach of duty in neglecting to do so; though, if the husband had allowed her sufficient food for the apprentice, and she had wilfully withholden it from him, then she would have been guilty. But that here the fact was otherwise; and therefore, though *in foro conscientiæ* the wife was equally guilty with the husband, yet in point of law she could not be said to be guilty of not providing the apprentice with sufficient food and nourishment" (Ibid., pp. 144, 145). It is hard to see what advantage society gains by this curious fashion of reckoning married women as children or lunatics. Some advantages, however, flow to a criminal husband: a wife is not punishable for concealing her husband from justice, knowing that he has committed felony; a husband may not conceal his wife under analogous circumstances: "So strict is the law where a felony is actually complete, in order to do effectual justice, that the nearest relations are not suffered to aid or receive one another. If the parent assists his child, or the child his parent, if the brother receives the brother, the master his servant, or the servant his master, or even if the husband receives his wife, having any of them committed a felony, the receiver becomes an accessory *ex post facto*. But a *feme covert* cannot become an accessory by the receipt and concealment of her husband; for she is presumed to act under his coercion, and therefore she is not bound, neither ought she, to discover her lord" (Ibid., p. 38). The wife of a blind husband must not, however, regard her coverture as in all cases a protection, for it has been held that if stolen goods were in her possession, her husband's blindness preventing him from knowing of them, her coverture did not avail to shelter her.

Any advantage which married women may possess through

the supposition that they are acting under the coercion of their husbands ought to be summarily taken away from them. It is not for the safety of society that criminals should escape punishment simply because they happen to be married women; a criminal husband becomes much more dangerous to the community if he is to have an irresponsible fellow-conspirator beside him; two people—although the law regards them as one—can often commit a crime that a single person could not accomplish, and it is not even impossible that an unscrupulous woman, desiring to get rid easily for awhile of an unpleasant husband, might actually be the secret prompter of an offence, in the commission of which she might share, but in the punishment of which she would have no part. For the sake of wives, as well as of husbands, this irresponsibility should be put an end to, for if a husband is to be held accountable for his wife's misdeeds and debts, it is impossible for the law to refuse him control over her actions; freedom and responsibility must go hand in hand, and women who obtain the rights of freedom must accept the duties of responsibility.

A woman has a legal claim on her husband for the necessaries of life, and a man may be compelled to support his wife. But her claim is a very narrow one, as may be seen by the following case:—A man named Plummer was indicted for the manslaughter of his wife; he had been separated from her for several years, and paid her an allowance of 2s. 6d. a week; the last payment was made on a Sunday, and she was turned out of her lodgings on the Tuesday following; she was suffering from diarrhœa, and on the Wednesday was very ill. Plummer was told of her condition, but refused to give her shelter; the evening was wet, and a constable meeting her wandering about took her to her husband's lodgings, but he would not admit her; on Thursday he paid for a bed for her at a public-house, and on Friday she died. Baron Gurney told the jury that the prisoner could not be charged with having caused her death from want of food, since he made her an allowance, and under ordinary circumstances he might have refused to do anything more; the only question was whether the refusal as to shelter had hastened her death. The man was acquitted. A wife has also some limited rights over her husband's property after his death; she may claim dower, her wearing apparel, a bed, and some few other things, including her personal jewellery. Her husband's power to deprive her of her personal ornaments ceases with his life.

To redress the whole of the wrongs as to property, and to enable justice to be done, it is only necessary to pass a short Act of Parliament, ordaining that marriage shall in no fashion alter the civil status of a woman, that she shall have over property the same rights as though she were unmarried, and shall, in all civil and criminal matters, be held as responsible as though she were a *feme sole.* In short, marriage ought no more to affect a woman's position than it does a man's, and should carry with it no kind of legal disability; "marital control" should cease to exist, and marriage should be regarded as a contract between equals, and not as a bond between master and servant.

Those who are entirely opposed to the idea that a woman should not forfeit her property on marriage, raise a number of theoretical difficulties as to household expenses, ownership of furniture, &c., &c. Practically these would very seldom occur, if we may judge by the experience of countries whose marriage laws do not entail forfeiture on the woman who becomes a wife. In the "Rights of Women," quoted from above, a very useful summary is given of the laws as to property in various countries; in Germany these laws vary considerably in the different states; one system, known as "Gütergemeinschaft" (community of goods) is a great advance towards equality, although it is not by any means the best resolution of the problem; under this system there is no separate property, it is all merged in the common stock, and "the husband, as such, has no more right over the common fund than the wife, nor the wife than the husband" (p. 26); the husband administers as "representative of the community, and not as husband. He is merely head partner, as it were, and has no personal rights beyond that;" he may be dispossessed of even this limited authority if he is wasteful; "he cannot alienate or mortgage any of the common lands or rights without her consent—a privilege, it must be remembered, which belongs to her, not only over lands brought by herself, but also over those brought by her husband to the marriage. And this control of the wife over the immovables has, for parts of Prussia, been extended by a law of April 16th, 1850, over movables as well; for the husband has been forbidden to dispose not only of immovables, but of the whole or part of the movable property, without the consent of his wife. Nor can the husband by himself make donations *mortis causa;* such arrangements take the form of mutual agreements between the two respecting their claims of inheritance to one another" (p. 27). In Austria, married couples are more independent of each other; the wives retain their rights over their own property, and can dispose of it "as they like, and sue or be sued in respect of it, without marital authorisation or control; and just as they have the free disposition of their property, so they can contract with others as they please. A husband is unable to alienate any of his wife's property in her name, or to lend or mortgage it, or to receive any money, institute any law-suits, or make any arrangements in respect of it, unless he has her special mandate. . . . If no stipulation is made at the marriage, each spouse retains his or her separate property, and neither has a claim to anything gained or in any way received by the other during the marriage" (p. 50). In the New York code (U.S.A.), "beyond the claim of mutual support, neither [husband nor wife] has any interest whatever in the property of the other. Hence either may into any enter engagement or transaction with the other or with a stranger with respect to property, just as they might do if they continued unmarried" (p. 95). The apportionment of household expenses must necessarily be left for the private arrangement of the married pair; where the woman has property, or where she earns her livelihood it would be her duty to contribute to the support of the common home; where the couple are poor, and the care of the house falls directly on the shoulders of the wife, her personal toil would be her fair contribution; this matter should be arranged in the marriage contract, just as similar matters are now dealt with in the marriage settlements of the wealthy. As means of livelihood become more accessible to women the question will be more and more easily arranged; it will no longer be the fashion in homes of professional men that the husband shall over-work himself in earning the means of support, while the wife over-rests herself in spending them, but a more evenly-divided duty shall strengthen the husband's health by more leisure, and the wife's by more work. Recovery of debts incurred for household expenses should be by suit against husband and wife jointly, just as in a partnership the firm may now be sued; recovery of personal debts should be by suits against the person who had contracted them. Many a man's life is now rendered harder than it ought to be, by the waste and extravagance of a wife who can pledge his name and his credit, and even ruin him before he knows his danger:

would not the lives of such men be the happier and the less toilsome if their wives were responsible for their own debts, and limited by their own means? Many a woman's home is broken up, and her children beggared, by the reckless spendthrift who wastes her fortune or her earnings: would not the lives of such women be less hopeless, if marriage left their property in their own hands, and did not give them a master as well as a husband? Women, under these circumstances, would, of course, become liable for the support of their children, equally with their husbands—a liability which is, indeed, recognized by the Married Women's Property Act (1870), s. 14.

It is sometimes further urged by those who like "a man to be master in his own house," that unless women forfeited their property in marriage, there would be constant discord in the home. Surely the contrary effect would be produced. Mrs. Mill well says, in the Essay before quoted from: "The highest order of durable and happy attachments would be a hundred times more frequent than they are, if the affection which the two sexes sought from one another were that genuine friendship which only exists between equals in privileges as in faculties." Nothing is so likely to cause unhappiness as the tendency to tyrannize, generated in the man by authority, and the tendency to rebel, generated in the woman by enforced submission. No grown person should be under the arbitrary power of another; dependence is touching in the infant because of its helplessness; it is revolting in the grown man or woman because with maturity of power should come dignity of self-support.

In a brilliant article in the *Westminster Review* (July, 1874) the writer well says: "Would it not, to begin with, be well to instruct girls that weakness, cowardice, and ignorance, cannot constitute at once the perfection of womankind and the imperfection of mankind?" It is time to do away with the oak and ivy ideal, and to teach each plant to grow strong and self-supporting. Perfect equality would, under this system, be found in the home, and mutual respect and deference would replace the alternate coaxing and commandment now too often seen. Equal rights would abolish both tyranny and rebellion; there would be more courtesy in the husband, more straightforwardness in the wife. Then, indeed, would there be some hope of generally happy marriages, but, as has been eloquently said by the writer just quoted, "till absolute social and legal equality is the basis of the sacred partnership of marriage (the division of labours and duties in the family, by free agreement, implying no sort of inequality), till no superiority is recognized on either side but that of individual character and capacity, till marriage is no longer legally surrounded with penalties on the woman who enters into it as though she were a criminal—till then the truest love, the truest sympathy, the truest happiness in it, will be the exception rather than the rule, and the real value of this relation, domestic and social, will be fatally missed." That some marriages are happy, in spite of the evil law, no one will deny; but these are the exception, not the rule. The law, as it is, directly tends to promote unhappiness, and its whole influence on the relations of the sexes is injurious. To quote Mrs. Mill once more: "The influence of the position tends eminently to promote selfishness. The most insignificant of men, the man who can obtain influence or consideration nowhere else, finds one place where he is chief and head. There is one person, often greatly his superior in understanding, who is obliged to consult him, and whom he is not obliged to consult. He is judge, magistrate, ruler, over their joint concerns; arbiter of all differences between them. . . . His is now the only tribunal, in civilized life, in which the same person is judge and party. A generous mind in such a situation makes the balance incline against its own side, and gives the other not less, but more, than a fair equality, and thus the weaker side may be enabled to turn the very fact of dependence into an instrument of power, and in default of justice, take an ungenerous advantage of generosity; rendering the unjust power, to those who make an unselfish use of it, a torment and a burthen. But how is it when average men are invested with this power, without reciprocity and without responsibility? Give such a man the idea that he is first in law and in opinion—that to will is his part, and hers to submit—it is absurd to suppose that this idea merely glides over his mind, without sinking into it, or having any effect on his feelings and practice. If there is any self-will in the man, he becomes either the conscious or unconscious despot of his household. The wife, indeed, often succeeds in gaining her objects, but it is by some of the many various forms of indirectness and management." When marriage is as it should be, there will be no superior and inferior by right of position; but men and women, whether married or unmarried, will retain intact the natural rights "belonging to every Englishman."

In dealing with the wrongs of the wife, according to the present English marriage laws, the wrongs of the mother must not be omitted. The unmarried mother has a right to her child; the married mother has none: "A father is entitled to the custody of his child until it attains the age of sixteen, unless there be some sufficient reason to the contrary" (Russell "On Crimes," vol. i., p. 898). The "sufficient reason" is hard to find in most cases, as the inclination of the Courts is to make excuses for male delinquencies, and to uphold every privilege which male Parliaments have conferred on husbands and fathers. In Shelley's case the father was deprived of the custody of his children, but here religious and political heresy caused a strong bias against the poet. The father's right to the custody of legitimate children is complete; the mother has no right over them as against his; he may take them away from her, and place them in the care of another woman, and she has no redress; she may apply to Chancery for access to them at stated times, but even this is matter of favour, not of right. The father may appoint a guardian in his will, and the mother, although the sole surviving parent, has no right over her children as against the stranger appointed by the dead father. If the parents differ in religion, the children are to be brought up in that of the father, whatever agreement may have been made respecting them before marriage; if the father dies without leaving any directions, the children will be educated in his religion; he can, if he chooses, allow his wife to bring them up in her creed, but she can only do so by virtue of his permission. Thus the married mother has no rights over her own children; she bears them, nurses them, toils for them, watches over them, and may then have them torn from her by no fault of her own, and given into the care of a stranger. People talk of maternal love, and of woman's sphere, of her duty in the home, of her work for her babes, but the law has no reverence for the tie between mother and child, and ignores every claim of the mother who is also a wife. The unmarried mother is far better off; she has an absolute right to the custody of her own children; none can step in and deprive her of her little ones, for the law respects the maternal tie when no marriage ceremony has "legitimated" it. Motherhood is only sacred in the eye of the law when no legal contract exists between the parents of the child.

Looking at a woman's position both as wife and mother, it is impossible not to recognise the fact that marriage is a direct disadvantage to her. In an unlegalised union the woman retains possession of all her natural rights; she is mistress of her own actions, of her body, of her property; she is able to legally defend herself against attack; all the Courts are open to protect her; she forfeits none of her rights as an Englishwoman; she keeps intact her liberty and her independence; she has no master; she owes obedience to the laws alone. If she have a child, the law acknowledges her rights over it, and no man can use her love for it as an engine of torture to force her into compliance with his will. Two disadvantages, however, attach to unlegalised unions; first, the woman has to face social disapprobation, although of late years, as women have been coming more to the front, this difficulty has been very much decreased, for women have begun to recognise the extreme injustice of the laws, and both men and women of advanced views have advocated great changes in the marriage contract. The second disadvantage is of a more serious character: the children proceeding from an unlegalised union have not the same rights as those born in legal wedlock, do not inherit as of right, and have no legal name. These injustices can be prevented by care in making testamentary dispositions protecting them, and by registering the surname, but the fact of the original unfairness still remains, and any carelessness on the parents' part will result in real injury to the child. It must also be remembered that the father, in such a case, has no rights over his children, and this is as unfair to him as the reverse is to the mother. As the law now is, both legal and illegal unions have disadvantages connected with them, and there is only a choice between evils; these evils are, however, overwhelmingly greater on the side of legal unions, as may be seen by the foregoing sketch of the disabilities imposed on women by marriage. So great are these that no wise and self-respecting woman should, with her eyes open, enter into a contract of marriage while the laws remain as they are, and no man who really honours a woman should ask her to subject herself to the disadvantages imposed on the English wife, or should ask her to take him as literally her master and owner. The relative position is as dishonouring to the man as it is insulting to the woman, and good men revolt against it as hotly as do the most high-spirited women. In happy marriages all these laws are ignored, and it is only at rare intervals that the married pair become conscious of their existence. Some argue that this being so, small practical harm results from the legal injustice; it would be as sensible to argue that as honest people do not want to thieve, it would not be injurious to public morality to have laws on the statute book legalising garotting. Laws are made to prevent injustice being committed with impunity, and it is a curious reversal of every principle of legislation to make laws which protect wrong-doing, and which can only be defended on the ground that they are not generally enforced. If the English marriage laws were universally carried out, marriage would not last for a month in England; as it is, vast numbers of women suffer in silence, thousands rebel and break their chains, and on every side men and women settle down into a mutual tolerance which is simply an easy-going indifference, accepted as the only possible substitute for the wedded happiness which they once dreamed of in youth, but have failed to realise in their maturity.

Things being as they are, what is the best action for those to take who desire to see a healthier and purer sexual morality—a morality founded upon equal rights and diverse duties harmoniously discharged? The first step is to agitate for a reform of the marriage laws by the passing of such an Act of Parliament as is alluded to above. It would be well for some of those who desire to see such a legislative change to meet and confer together on the steps to be taken to introduce such a Bill into the House of Commons. If thought necessary, a Marriage Reform League might be established, to organize the agitation and petitioning which are *de rigueur*, in endeavouring to get a bill passed through the popular House. Side by side with this effort to reform marriage abuses, should go the determination not to contract a legal marriage while the laws remain as immoral as they are. It is well known that the Quakers persistently refused to go through the legal English form of marriage, and quietly made their declarations according to their own conscience, submitting to the disadvantages entailed on them by the illegality, until the legislature formally recognised the Quaker declaration as a legal form of marriage. Why should not we take a leaf out of the Quakers' book, and substitute for the present legal forms of marriage a simple declaration publicly made? We should differ from the Quakers in this, that we should not desire that such declaration should be legalised while the marriage laws remain as they are; but as soon as the laws are moralised, and wives are regarded as self-possessing human beings, instead of as property, then the declaration may, with advantage, seek the sanction of the law. It is not necessary that the declaration should be couched in any special form of words; the conditions of the contract ought to be left to the contracting parties. What is necessary is that it should be a definite contract, and it is highly advisable that it should be a contract in writing—a deed of partnership, in fact, which should — when the law permits—be duly stamped and registered. The law, while it does not dictate the conditions of the contract, should enforce those conditions so long as the contract exists; that is, it should interfere just as far as it does in other contracts, and no further; the law has no right to dictate the terms of the marriage contract; it is for the contracting parties to arrange their own affairs as they will. While, however, the province of the law should be thus limited in respect to the contracting parties, it has a clear right to interfere in defence of the interests of any children who may be born of the marriage, and to compel the parents to clothe, feed, house, and educate them properly: this duty should, if need be, be enforced on both parents alike, and the law should recognise and impose the full discharge of the responsibilities of parents towards those to whom they have given life. No marriage contract should be recognised by the law which is entered into by minors; in this, as in other legal deeds, there should be no capability to contract until the contracting parties are of full age. A marriage is a partnership, and should be so regarded by the law, and it should be the aim of those who are endeavouring to reform marriage, to substitute for the present semi-barbarous laws a scheme which shall be sober, dignified, and practicable, and which shall recognise the vital interest of the community in the union of those who are to be the parents of the next generation.

Such a deed as I propose would have no legal force at the present time; and here arises a difficulty: might not a libertine take advantage of this fact to desert his wife and possibly leave her with a child, or children, on her hands, to the cold mercy of society which would not even recognize her as a married woman? Men who, under the present state of the law, seduce women and then desert them, would probably do the same if they had gone through a form of marriage which had no legally binding force; but such men are, fortunately, the exception, not the rule, and there is no reason to apprehend an increase of their number, owing to the proposed action on the part of a number of thoughtful men and women who are dissatisfied with the present state of the law, but who have no wish to plunge into debauchery. I freely acknowledge that it is to be desired that marriage should be legally binding, and that a father should be compelled to do his share towards supporting his children; but while English law imposes such a weight of disability on a married woman, and leaves her utterly in the power of her husband, however unprincipled, oppressive, and wicked he may be—short of legal crime—I take leave to think that women have a fairer chance of happiness and comfort in an unlegalised than in a legal marriage. There is many an unhappy woman who would be only too glad if the libertine who has legally married her would desert her, and leave her, even with the burden of a family, to make for herself and her children, by her own toil, a home which should at least be pure, peaceful, and respectable.

Let me, in concluding this branch of the subject, say a word to those who, agreeing with Marriage Reform in principle, fear to openly put their theory into practice. Some of these earnestly hope for change, but do not dare to advocate it openly. Reforms have never been accomplished by Reformers who had not the courage of their opinions. If all the men and women who disapprove of the present immoral laws would sturdily *and openly* oppose them; if those who desire to unite their lives, but are determined not to submit to the English marriage laws, would publicly join hands, making such a declaration as is here suggested, the social odium would soon pass away, and the unlegalised marriage would be recognised as a dignified and civilized substitute for the old brutal and savage traditions. Most valuable work might here be done by men and women who—happy in their own marriages—yet feel the immorality of the law, and desire to see it changed. Such married people might support and strengthen by their open countenance and friendship those who enter into the unlegalised public unions here advocated; and they can do what no one else can do so well: they can prove to English society—the most bigoted and conservative society in the world—that advocacy of change in the marriage laws does not mean the abolition of the home. The value of such co-operation will be simply inestimable, and will do more than anything else to render the reform practicable. Courage and quiet resolution are needed, but, with these, this great social change may safely and speedily be accomplished.

II.

DIVORCE.

Any proposed reforms in the marriage laws of England would be extremely imperfect, unless they dealt with the question of divorce. Marriage differs from all ordinary contracts in the extreme difficulty of dissolving it—a difficulty arising from the ecclesiastical character which has been imposed upon it, and from the fact that it has been looked upon as a religious bond instead of as a civil contract. Until the time of the Reformation, marriage was regarded as a sacrament by all Christian people, and it is so regarded by the majority of them up to the present day. When the Reformers advocated divorce, it was considered as part of their general heresy, and as proof of the immoral tendency of their doctrines. Among Roman Catholics the sacramental—and therefore the indissoluble—character of marriage is still maintained, but among Protestants divorce is admitted, the laws regulating it varying much in different countries.

In England—owing to the extreme conservatism of the English in all domestic matters—the Protestant view of marriage made its way very slowly. Divorce remained within the jurisdiction of ecclesiastical courts, and these granted only divorces *a mensâ et thoro* in cases where cruelty or adultery was pleaded as rendering conjugal life impossible. These courts never granted divorces *a vinculo matrimonii*, which permit either—or both—of the divorced persons to contract a fresh marriage, except in cases where the marriage was annulled as having been void from the beginning; they would only grant a separation "from bed and board," and imposed celibacy on the divorced couple until one of them died, and so set the other free. There was indeed a report drawn up by a commission, under the authority of 3 and 4 Edward VI., c. ii., which was intended as a basis for the re-modelling of the marriage laws, but the death of the king prevented the proposed reform; the ecclesiastical courts remained as they were, and absolute divorce was unattainable. Natural impatience of a law which separated unhappy married people only to impose celibacy on them, caused occasional applications to be made to Parliament for relief, and a few marriages were thus dissolved under exceptional circumstances. In 1701, a bill was obtained, enabling a petitioner to re-marry, and in 1798, Lord Loughborough's "Orders" were passed. "By these orders, no petition could be presented to the House, unless an official copy of the proceedings, and of a definitive sentence of divorce, *a mensâ et thoro*, in the ecclesiastical courts, was delivered on oath at the bar of the House at the same time" (Broom's "Comm.," vol. iii. p. 396). After explaining the procedure of the ecclesiastical court, Broom goes on: "A definitive sentence of divorce *a mensâ et thoro* being thus obtained, the petitioner proceeded to lay his case before the House of Lords in accordance with the Standing Orders before adverted to, and, subject to his proving the case, he obtained a bill divorcing him from the bonds of matrimony, and allowing him to marry again. The provisions of the bill, which was very short, were generally these:—1. The marriage was dissolved. 2. The husband was empowered to marry again. 3. He was given the rights of a husband as to any property of an after-taken wife. 4. The divorced wife was deprived of any right she might have as his widow. 5. Her after-acquired property was secured to her as against the husband from whom she was divorced. In the case of the wife obtaining the bill, similar provisions were made in her favour" (p. 398). In 1857, an Act was passed establishing a Court for Divorce and Matrimonial Causes, and thus a great step forward was taken: this court was empowered to grant a judicial separation—equivalent to the old divorce *a mensâ et thoro*—in cases of cruelty, desertion for two years and upwards, or adultery on the part of the husband; it was further empowered to grant an absolute divorce with right of re-marriage—equivalent to the old divorce *a vinculo matrimonii*—in cases of adultery on the part of the wife, or of, on the part of the husband, "incestuous adultery, or of bigamy with adultery, or of rape, or an unnatural crime, or of adultery coupled with such cruelty as would formerly have entitled her to a divorce *a mensâ et thoro*, or of adultery coupled with desertion, without reasonable excuse, for two years or upwards"

(Broom, vol. i., p. 542). The other powers held by the court need not now be specially dwelt upon.

The first reform here needed is that husband and wife should be placed on a perfect equality in asking for a divorce: at present if husband and wife be living apart, no amount of adultery on the husband's part can release the wife; if they be living together, a husband may keep as many mistresses as he will, and, provided that he carefully avoid any roughness which can be construed into legal cruelty, he is perfectly safe from any suit for dissolution of marriage. Adultery alone, when committed by the husband, is not ground for a dissolution of marriage; it must be coupled with some additional offence before the wife can obtain her freedom. But the husband can obtain a dissolution of marriage for adultery committed by the wife, and he can further obtain money damages from the co-respondent, as a *solatium* to his wounded feelings. Divorce should be absolutely equal as between husband and wife: adultery on either side should be sufficient, and if it be thought necessary to join a male co-respondent when the husband is the injured party, then it should also be necessary to join a female co-respondent where the wife brings the suit. The principle, then, which should be laid down as governing all cases of divorce, is that no difference should be made in favour of either side; whatever is sufficient to break the marriage in the one case should be sufficient to break it in the other.

Next, the system of judicial separation should be entirely swept away. Wherever divorce is granted at all, the divorce should be absolute. No useful end is gained by divorcing people practically and regarding them as married legally. A technical tie is kept up, which retains on the wife the mass of disabilities which flow from marriage, while depriving her of all the privileges, and which widows both man and woman, exiling them from home-life and debarring them from love. Judicial separation is a direct incentive to licentiousness and secret sexual intercourse; the partially divorced husband, refused any recognised companion, either indulges in promiscuous lust, to the ruin of his body and mind, or privately lives with some woman whom the law forbids him to marry and whom he is ashamed to openly acknowledge. Meanwhile the semi-divorced wife can obtain no relief, and is compelled to live on, without the freedom of the spinster or the widow, or the social consideration of the married woman. She can only obtain freedom by committing what the law and society brand as adultery; if she has any scruples on this head, she must remain alone, unloved and without home, living a sad, solitary life until death, more merciful than the law, sets her free.

It is hard to see what object there can be in separating a married couple, in breaking up the home, dividing the children, and yet maintaining the fact of marriage just so far as shall prevent the separated couple from forming new ties; the position of those who regard divorce as altogether sinful, is intelligible, however mistaken; but the position of those who advocate divorce, but object to the divorced couple having the right of contracting a new marriage, is wholly incomprehensible. No one profits by such divorce, while the separated couple are left in a dubious and most unsatisfactory condition; they are neither married nor unmarried; they can never shake themselves free from the links of the broken chain; they carry about with them the perpetual mark of their misfortune, and can never escape from the blunder committed in their youth. They would be the happier, and society would be the healthier, if the divorce of life and of interests were also a divorce which should set them free to seek happiness, if they will, in other unions—free technically as well as really, free in law as well as in fact.

If it be admitted that all divorce should be absolute, the question arises: What should be the ground of divorce? First, adultery, because breach of faith on either side should void the contract which implies loyalty to each other; the legal costs of both should fall on the breaker of the contract, but no damages should be recoverable against a third party. Next, cruelty, because where the weaker party suffers from the abuse of power of the stronger, there the law should, when appealed to, step in to annul the contract, which is thus a source of injury to one of the contracting parties; if a man be brought up before the magistrate charged with wife-beating or violence of any kind towards his wife, and be convicted and sentenced, the Divorce Court should, on the demand of the wife, the record being submitted to it, pronounce a sentence of divorce; in the rare case of violence committed by a wife on her husband, the same result should accrue; the custody of the children should be awarded to the innocent party, since neither a man nor a woman convicted of doing bodily harm to another is fit to be trusted with the guardianship of a child.* The next distinct ground of divorce should be habitual drunkenness; drunkenness causes misery to the sober partner, and is ruinous in its effect, both on the *physique* and on the character of the children proceeding from the marriage. Here, of course, the custody of the children should be committed entirely to the innocent parent.

At present, the usual unfairness presides over the arrangements as to access to the children by the parents: "In the case of a mother who is proved guilty of adultery, she is usually debarred from such access, though it has not been the practice to treat the offending father with the same rigour" (Broom's "Comm.," vol. iii., p. 404). In all cases of divorce the interests of the children should be carefully guarded; both parents should be compelled to contribute to their support, whether the guardianship be confided to the father or to the mother.

These glaring reasons for granting a divorce will be admitted by everyone who recognises the reasonableness of divorce at all, but there will be more diversity of opinion as to the advisability of making divorce far more easily attainable. The French Convention of 1792 set an example that has been only too little followed; for the first time in French history divorce was legalised in France. It was obtainable "on the application of either party [to the marriage] alleging simply as a cause, incompatibility of humour or character. The female children were to be entirely confided to the care of the mother, as well as the males, to the age of seven years, when the latter were again to be re-committed to the superintendence of the father; provided only, that by mutual agreement any other arrangement might take place with respect to the disposal of the children; or arbitrators might be chosen by the nearest of kin to determine on the subject. The parents were to contribute equally to the maintenance of the children, in proportion to their property, whether under the care of the father or mother. Family arbitrators were to be chosen to direct with respect to the partition of the property, or the alimentary pension to be allowed to the party divorced. Neither of the parties

* Since these lines were published in the *National Reformer*, a clause has been inserted in a bill now before Parliament, empowering magistrates to grant an order of separation to a wife, if it is proved that she has been cruelly ill-used by her husband, and further compelling the husband, in such a case, to contribute a weekly sum towards her maintenance. This will be a great improvement on the present state of things, but absolute divorce would be better than mere separation.

could contract a new marriage for the space of one year" ("Impartial History of the Late Revolution," vol. ii., pp. 179, 180). This beneficial law was swept away, with many other useful changes, when tyranny came back to France. At the present time the only countries where divorce is easily obtainable are some of the states of Germany and of America. It has been held in at least one American state that proved incompatibility of temper was sufficient ground for separation. And reasonably so; if two people enter into a contract for their mutual comfort and advantage, and the contract issues in mutual misery and loss, why should not the contract be dissolved? It is urged that marriage would be dishonoured if divorce were easily attainable; surely marriage is far more dishonoured by making it a chain to tie together two people who have for each other neither affection nor respect. For the sake of everyone concerned an unhappy marriage should be easily dissoluble; the married couple would be the happier and the better for the separation; their children—if they have any—would be saved from the evil effect of continual family jars, and from the loss of respect for their parents caused by the spectacle of constant bickering; the household would be spared the evil example of the quarrels of its heads; society would see less vice and fewer scandalous divorce suits. In all cases of contract, save that of marriage, those who make can, by mutual consent, unmake; why should those who make the most important contract of all be deprived of the same right?

Mr. John Stuart Mill, dealing very briefly with the marriage contract in his essay "On Liberty," points out that the fulfilment of obligations incurred by marriage must not be forgotten when the contract is dissolved, since these "must be greatly affected by the continuance or disruption of the relation between the original parties to the contract." But he goes on to say: "It does not follow, nor can I admit, that these obligations extend to requiring the fulfilment of the contract at all costs to the happiness of the reluctant party; but they are a necessary element in the question; and even if, as Von Humboldt maintains, they ought to make no difference in the *legal* freedom of the parties to release themselves from the engagement (and I also hold that they ought not to make *much* difference), they necessarily make a great difference in the *moral* freedom. A person is bound to take all these circumstances into account before resolving on a step which may affect such important interests of others; and if he does not allow proper weight to those interests, he is morally responsible for the wrong. I have made these obvious remarks for the better illustration of the general principle of liberty, and not because they are at all needed on the particular question, which, on the contrary, is usually discussed as if the interest of children was everything, and that of grown persons nothing" (p. 61). The essay of Von Humboldt, referred to by Mr. Mill, is that on the "Sphere and Duties of Government;" Von Humboldt argues that "even where there is nothing to be objected to the validity of a contract, the State should have the power of lessening the restrictions which men impose on one another, even with their own consent, and (by facilitating the release from such engagements) of preventing a moment's decision from hindering their freedom of action for too long a period of life" (p. 134, of Coulthard's translation). After pointing out that contracts relating to the transfer of *things* should be binding, Von Humboldt proceeds: "With contracts which render personal performance a duty, or still more with those which produce proper personal relations, the case is wholly different. With these coercion operates hurtfully on man's noblest powers; and since the success of the pursuit itself which is to be conducted in accordance with the contract, is more or less dependent on the continuing consent of the parties, a limitation of such a kind is in them productive of less serious injury. When, therefore, such a personal relation arises from the contract as not only to require certain single actions, but, in the strictest sense, to affect the person, and influence the whole manner of his existence; where that which is done, or left undone, is in the closest dependence on internal sensations, the option of separation should always remain open, and the step itself should not require any extenuating reasons. Thus it is with matrimony" (pp. 134, 135).

Robert Dale Owen—the virtuous and justly revered author of "Moral Physiology;" a man so respected in his adopted country, the United States of America, that he was elected as one of its senators, and was appointed American ambassador at the Court of Naples—Robert Dale Owen, in a letter to Thomas Whittemore, editor of the Boston *Trumpet*, May, 1831, deals as follows with the contract of marriage:—

"I do not think it virtuous or rational in a man and woman solemnly to swear that they will love and honour each other until death part them. First, because if affection or esteem on either side should afterwards cease (as, alas! we often see it cease), the person who took the marriage-oath has perjured himself; secondly, because I have observed that such an oath, being substituted for the noble and elevating principle of moral obligation, has a tendency to weaken that principle.

"You will probably ask me whether I should equally object to a solemn promise to live together during life whatever happens. I do not think this *equally* objectionable, because it is an explicit promise possible to be kept; whereas the oath to love until death, may become impossible of fulfilment. But still I do not approve even this possible promise; and I will give you the reasons why I do not.

"That a man and woman should occupy the same house, and daily enjoy each other's society, so long as such an association gives birth to virtuous feelings, to kindness, to mutual forbearance, to courtesy, to disinterested affection, I consider right and proper. That they should continue to inhabit the same house and to meet daily, in case such intercourse should give birth to vicious feelings, to dislike, to ill temper, to scolding, to a carelessness of each other's comfort and a want of respect for each other's feelings,—this I consider, *when the two individuals alone are concerned*, neither right nor proper; neither conducive to good order nor to virtue. I do not think it well, therefore, to promise, at all hazards, to live together for life.

"Such a view may be offensive to orthodoxy, but surely, surely it is approved by common sense. Ask yourself, sir, who is—who can be the gainer—the man, the woman, or society at large—by two persons living in discord rather than parting in peace, as Abram and Lot did when their herdsmen could not agree. We have temptations enough already to ill humour in the world, without expressly creating them for ourselves; and of all temptations to that worst of petty vices, domestic bickering, can we suppose one more strong or more continually active than a forced association in which the heart has no share? Do not the interests of virtue and good order, then, imperiously demand (as the immortal author of 'Paradise Lost' argued, in his celebrated work 'On Divorce,') that the law should abstain from perpetuating any association, after it has become a daily source of vice?

"If children's welfare is concerned, and that they will be injured by a separation, the case is different. Those who impart existence to sentient beings are, in my view, responsible to them for as much happiness as it is in their power to bestow. The parent voluntarily assumes this greatest of responsibilities; and he who, having so assumed it, trifles with his child's best interests for his own selfish gratification, is, in my eyes, utterly devoid of moral principle; or, at the least, utterly blind to the most sacred duty which a human being can be called to perform. If, therefore, the well-being and future prosperity of the children are to be sacrificed by a separation of the parents, then I would positively object to the separation, however grievous the evil effects of a continued connection might be to the dissentient couple.

"Whether the welfare of children is ever promoted by the continuation of an ill-assorted union, is another question; as also in what way they ought to be provided for, where a separation actually takes place.

"But to regard, for the moment, the case of the adults alone. You will remark, that it is no question for us to determine whether it is better or more proper that affection, once conceived, should last through life. We might as well sit down to decree whether the sun should shine or be hid under a cloud, or whether the wind should blow a storm or a gentle breeze. We may rejoice when it does so last, and grieve when it does not; but as to legislating about the matter, it is the idlest of absurdities.

"But we *can* determine by law the matter of living together. We may compel a man and woman, though they hate each other as cordially as any of Byron's heroes, to have one common name, one common interest, and (nominally) one common bed and board. We may invest them with the legal appearance of the closest friends while they are the bitterest enemies. It seems to me that mankind have seldom considered what are the actual advantages of such a proceeding to the individuals and to society. I confess that I do not see what is gained in so unfortunate a situation, by keeping up the appearance when the reality is gone.

"I do see the necessity, in such a case, if the man and woman separate, of dividing what property they may possess equally between them; and (while the present monopoly of profitable occupations by men lasts) I also see the expei en cy, in case the property so divided be not sufficient for the woman's comfortable support, of causing the man to continue to contribute a fair proportion of his earnings towards it. I also see the impropriety, as I said before, that the children, if any there be, should suffer. But I cannot see who is the gainer by obliging two persons to continue in each other's society, when heart-burnings, bickerings, and other vicious results, are to be the consequence.

"There are cases when affection ceases on one side and remains on the other. No one can deny that this is an evil, often a grievous one; but I cannot perceive how the law can remedy it, or soften its bitterness, any more than it can legislate away the pain caused by unreturned friendship between persons of the same sex.

"You will ask me, perhaps, whether I do not believe that, but for the law, there would be a continual and selfish change indulged, without regard to the feelings or welfare of others. What there might be in the world, viciously trained and circumstanced as so many human beings now are, I know not, though I doubt whether things *could* be much worse than they are now; besides that no human power can legislate for the heart. But if men and women were trained (as they so easily might!) to be even decently regardful of each other's feelings, may we not assert positively, that no such result could possibly happen? Let me ask each one of your readers, and let each answer to his or her own heart: 'Are you indeed bound to those you profess to love and honour by the law *alone?*' Alas! for your chance of happiness, if the answer be 'Yes!'"

The fact is, as Mr. Owen justly says, that a promise to "love . . . until death us do part" is an immoral promise, because its performance is beyond the power of those who give the promise. To love, or not to love, is not a matter of the will; Love in chains loses his life, and only leaves a corpse in his captive's hand. Love is, of its very nature, voluntary, freely given, drawing together by an irresistible sympathy those whose natures are adapted to each other. Shelley well says, in one of the notes on Queen Mab: "Love is inevitably consequent on the perception of loveliness. Love withers under constraint; its very essence is liberty; it is compatible neither with obedience, jealousy, nor fear; it is there most pure, perfect and unlimited, where its votaries live in confidence, equality, and unreserve." To say this, is not to say that higher duty may not come between the lovers, may not, for a time, keep them apart, may not even render their union impossible; it is only to recognize a fact that no thoughtful person can deny, and to show how utterly wrong and foolish it is to promise for life that which can never be controlled by the will.

But marriage, it is said, would be too lightly entered into if it were so easily dissoluble. Why? People do not rush into endless partnerships because they are dissoluble at pleasure; on the contrary, such partnerships last just so long as they are beneficial to the contracting parties. In the same way, marriage would last exactly so long as its continuance was beneficial, and no longer: when it became hurtful, it would be dissolved. "How long then," asks Shelley, "ought the sexual connection to last? what law ought to specify the extent of the grievances which should limit its duration? A husband and wife ought to continue so long united as they love each other; any law which should bind them to cohabitation for one moment after the decay of their affection, would be a most intolerable tyranny, and the most unworthy of toleration. How odious a usurpation of the right of private judgment should that law be considered which should make the ties of friendship indissoluble, in spite of the caprices, the inconstancy, the fallibility and capacity for improvement of the human mind. And by so much would the fetters of love be heavier and more unendurable than those of friendship, as love is more vehement and capricious, more dependent on those delicate peculiarities of imagination, and less capable of reduction to the ostensible merits of the object. . . . The connection of the sexes is so long sacred as it contributes to the comfort of the parties, and is naturally dissolved when its evils are greater than its benefits. There is nothing immoral in this separation" (Notes on "Queen Mab"). In spite of this facility of divorce, marriage would be the most enduring of all partnerships; not only is there between married couples the tie of sexual affection, but around them grows up a hedge of common thoughts, common interests, common memories, that, as years go on, makes the idea of separation more and more repulsive. It would only be where the distaste had grown strong enough to break through all these, that divorce would take place, and in such cases the misery of the enforced common life would be removed without harm to any one. Of course, this facility of divorce will entirely sweep away those odious suits for "restitution of conjugal rights" which occasionally disgrace our courts. If a husband and wife are living apart, without legal sanction, it is now open to either of them to bring a suit for restitution of conjugal rights. "The decree of restitution pronounces for the marriage, admonishes the respondent to take the petitioner home and treat him or her as husband or wife, and to render him or her conjugal rights; and, further, to certify to the court, within a certain time, that he or she had done so; in default of which, an attachment for contempt of court will be issued against the offending party" (Broom's "Comm.," vol. iii., p. 400). It is difficult to understand how any man or woman, endued with the most rudimentary sense of decency, can bring such a suit, and, after having succeeded, can enforce the decision. We may hope that, as sexual morality becomes more generally recognised, it will be seen that the essence of prostitution lies in the union of the sexes without mutual love; when a woman marries for rank, for title, for wealth, she sells herself as veritably as her poorer and more unfortunate sister; love alone makes the true marriage, love which is loyal to the beloved, and is swayed by no baser motive than passionate devotion to its object. When no such love exists the union which is marriage by law is nothing higher than legalised prostitution: the enforcement on an unwilling man or woman of conjugal rights is something even still lower, it is legalised rape.

It may be hoped that when divorce is more easily obtainable, the majority of marriages will be far happier than they are now. Half the unhappiness of married life arises from the too great feeling of security which grows out of the indissoluble character of the tie. The husband is very different from the lover; the wife from the betrothed; the ready attention, the desire to please, the eager courtesy, which characterised the lover disappear when possession has become certain; the daintiness, the gaiety, the attractiveness which marked the betrothed, are no longer to be seen in the wife whose position is secure; in society a lover may be known by his attention to his betrothed, a husband by his indifference to his wife. If divorce were the result of jarring at home, married life would very rapidly change; hard words, harshness, petulance, would be checked where those who had won the love desired to keep it, and attractiveness would no longer be dropped on the threshold of the home. Here, too, Shelley's words are well worth weighing: "The present system of restraint does no more, in the majority of instances, than make hypocrites or open enemies. Persons of delicacy and virtue, unhappily united to those whom they find it impossible to love, spend the loveliest season of their life in unproductive efforts to appear otherwise than they are, for the sake of the feelings of their partner, or the welfare of their mutual offspring; those of less generosity and refinement openly avow their disappointment, and linger out the remnant of that union, which only death can dissolve, in a state of incurable bickering and hostility. The early education of the children takes its colour from the squabbles of the parents; they are nursed in a systematic school of ill-humour, violence and falsehood. Had they been suffered to part at the moment when indifference rendered their union irksome, they would have been spared many years of misery: they would have connected themselves more suitably, and would have found that happiness in the society of more congenial partners which is for ever denied them by the despotism of marriage. They would have been separately useful and happy members of society, who, whilst united, were miserable, and rendered misanthropical by misery. The conviction that wedlock is indissoluble, holds out the strongest of all temptations to the perverse; they indulge without restraint in acrimony, and all the little tyrannies of domestic life, when they know that their victim is without appeal. If this conviction were put on a rational basis, each would be assured that habitual ill-temper would terminate in separation, and would check this vicious and dangerous propensity" (Notes on "Queen Mab"). To those who had thought over the subject carefully, it was no surprise to hear Mr. Moncure Conway say—in a debate on marriage at the Dialectical Society—that in Illinois, U.S.A., where there is great facility of divorce, the marriages were exceptionally happy. The reason was not far to seek.

Dealing elsewhere with this same injurious effect of over-certainty on the relations of married people to each other, Mr. Moncure Conway writes as follows:—"In England we smilingly walk our halls of Eblis, covering the fatal wound; but our neighbours across the Channel are frank. Their moralists cannot blot out the proverb that 'Marriage is the suicide of love.' Is it any truer here than there that, as a general thing, the courtesies of the courtship survive in the marriage? 'Who is that domino walking with George?' asks Grisette No. 1, as reported by *Charivari*. 'Why,' returns Grisette No. 2, 'do you not walk behind them, and listen to what they say?' 'I have done so, and they do not say a word.' 'Ah, it is his wife.' But what might be George's feeling if he knew his wife might leave him some morning? 'If conserve of roses be frequently eaten,' they say in Persia, 'it will produce a surfeit.' The thousands of husbands and wives yawning in each other's faces at this moment need not go so far for their proverb. If it be well, as it seems to me to be, that this most intimate relation between man and woman should be made as durable as the object for which it is formed will admit, surely the bond should be real to the last, a bond of kindliness, thoughtfulness, actual helpfulness. So long as the strength of the bond lies simply in the disagreeable concomitants of breaking it, so long as it is protected by the very iron hardness which makes it gall and oppress, what need is there of the reinforcement of it by the cultivation of minds, the preservation of good temper, and considerate behaviour? Love is not quite willing to accept the judge's mace for his arrow. When the law no longer supplies husband or wife with a cage, each must look to find and make available what resources he or she has for holding what has been won. We may then look for sober second thoughts both before and after marriage. Love, from so long having bandaged eyes, will be all eye. Every real attraction will be stimulated when all depends upon real attraction. When the conserve becomes fatiguing, it will be refreshed by a new flavour, not by a certificate. From the hour when a thought of obligation influences either party to it, the marriage becomes a prostitution." ("The Earthward Pilgrimage," pp. 289, 290, 291).

A remarkable instance of the permanence of unions dissoluble at pleasure is to be found related by Robert Dale Owen, in an article entitled "Marriage and Placement," which appeared in the *Free Inquirer* of May 28, 1831. It deals with the unions between the sexes in the Haytian Republic, and the facts therein related are well worthy of serious attention. Mr. Owen writes:—

"Legal marriage is common in St. Domingo as elsewhere. Prostitution, too, exists there as in other countries. But this institution of *placement* is found nowhere, that I know of, but among the Haytians.

"Those who choose to marry, are united, as in other countries, by a priest or magistrate. Those who do not choose to marry, and who equally shrink from the mercenary embrace of prostitution, are (in the phraseology of the island) *placés*: that is, literally translated, *placed.*

"The difference between *placement* and marriage is, that the former is entered into without any prescribed form, the latter with the usual ceremonies: the former is dissoluble at a day's warning, the latter is indissoluble except by the vexatious and degrading formalities of divorce; the former is a tacit social compact, the latter a legal compulsory one; in the former the woman gives up her name and her property; in the latter, she retains both.

"Marriage and placement are, in Hayti, equally respectable, or, if there be a difference, it is in favour of placement; and in effect ten placements take place in the island for one marriage. *Pétion*, the Jefferson of Hayti,* sanctioned the custom by his approval and example. *Boyer*, his successor, the president, did the same;† and by far the largest portion of the respectable inhabitants have imitated their presidents, and are *placed*, not married. The children of the placed have, in every particular, the same legal rights and the same standing as those born in wedlock.

"I imagine I hear from the clerical supporters of orthodoxy one general burst of indignation at this sample of national profligacy; at this contemning of the laws of God and man; at this escape from the Church's ceremonies and the ecclesiastical blessing. I imagine I hear the question sneeringly put, how long these same *respectable* connections commonly last, and how many dozen times they are changed in the course of a year.

"Gently, my reverend friends! it is natural you should find it wrong that men and women dispense with your services and curtail your fees in this matter. But it is neither just nor proper, that because no prayers are said, and no fees paid, you should denounce the custom as a profligate one. Learn (as I did the other day from an intelligent French

* "It may suffice, in illustration of Pétion's character, to quote the touching inscription found on his tomb—'Here lies Pétion, who enjoyed for twelve years absolute power, and during that period never caused one tear to flow.'"

† "Boyer's resolution in this matter is the more remarkable, as he has been urged and pestered to submit to the forms of marriage. Grégoire, archbishop of Blois, and who is well known for the perseverance and benevolence with which he has, for a long series of years, advocated the cause of the African race, wrote to the president of Hayti in the most urgent terms, pressing upon him the virtue—the necessity, for his salvation—of conforming to the sacrament of marriage. To such a degree did the good old archbishop carry his intermeddling officiousness, that when Boyer mildly but firmly declined availing himself of his grace's advice, a rupture was the consequence, greatly to the sorrow of the president, who had ever entertained the greatest respect and affection for his ecclesiastical friend."

gentleman who had remained some time on the island)—learn, that *although there are ten times as many placed as married, yet there are actually fewer separations among the former than divorces among the latter.* If constancy, then, is to be the criterion of morality, these same profligate unions—that is, unions unprayed-for by the priest and unpaid for to him—are ten times as moral as the religion-sanctioned institution of marriage.

"But this is not all. It is a fact notorious in Hayti, that libertinism is far more common among the married than among the placed. The explanatory cause is easily found. A placement secures to the consenting couple no *legal* right over one another. They remain together, as it were, on good behaviour. Not only positive tyranny or downright viragoism, but petulant peevishness or selfish ill humour, are sufficient causes of separation. As such, they are avoided with sedulous care. The natural consequence is, that the unions are usually happy, and that each being comfortable at home, is not on the search for excitement abroad. In indissoluble marriage, on the contrary, if the parties should happen to disagree, their first jarrings are unchecked by considerations of conquences. A husband may be as tyrannical as to him seems good; he remains a lord and master still; a wife may be as pettish as she pleases; she does not thereby forfeit the rights and privileges of a wife. Thus, ill humour is encouraged by being legalized, and the natural results ensue, alienation of the heart, and sundering of the affections. The wife seeks relief in fashionable dissipation; the husband, perhaps, in the brutalities of a brothel.

"But, aside from all explanatory theories, the FACT is, as I have stated it, viz.: that (taking the proportion of each into account) *there are ten legal separations of the married, for one voluntary separation of the placed.* If anyone doubts it, let him inquire for himself, and he will doubt no longer.

"What say you to that fact, my reverend friends? How consorts it with your favourite theory, that man is a profligate animal, a desperately wicked creature? that, but for your prayers and blessings, the earth would be a scene of licentiousness and excess? that human beings remain together, only because you have helped to tie them? that there is no medium between priestly marriage and unseemly prostitution?

"Does this fact open your eyes a little on the real state of things to which we heterodox spirits venture to look forward? Does it assist in explaining to you how it is that we are so much more willing than you to entrust the most sacred duties to moral rather than legal keeping?

"You cannot imagine that a man and a woman, finding themselves suited to each other, should agree, without your interference, to become companions; that he should remove to her plantation, or she to his, as they found it most convenient; that the connection should become known to their friends without the agency of banns, and be respected, even though not ostentatiously announced in a newspaper. Yet all this happens in Hayti, without any breach of propriety, without any increase of vice; but, on the contrary, much to the benefit of morality, and the discouragement of prostitution. It happens among the white as well as the coloured population; and the president of the country gives it his sanction, in his own person.

"Do you still ask me—accustomed as you are to consider virtue the offspring of restrictions—do you still ask me, what the checks are that produce and preserve such a state of things? I reply, good feeling and public opinion. Continual change is held to be disreputable; where sincere and well-founded affection exists, it is not desired; and as there is no pecuniary inducement in forming a placement, these voluntary unions are seldom ill-assorted."

Where social anarchy is feared, facts like these are worth pages of argument. If the Haytians are civilised enough for this more moral kind of marriage, why should Europeans be on a lower level? For it should not be forgotten that the experiment was tried in St. Domingo under great disadvantages, and these unlegalised unions have yet proved more permanent than those tied with all due formality and tightness.

It may be urged: if divorce is to be so easily attainable, why should there be a marriage contract at all? Both as regards the pair immediately concerned, and as regards the children who may result from the union, a clear and definite contract seems to me to be eminently desirable. It is not to be wished that the union of those on whom depends the next generation should be carelessly and lightly entered into; the dignity and self-recollection which a definite compact implies are by no means to be despised, when it is remembered how grave and weighty are the responsibilities assumed by those who are to give to the State new citizens, and to Humanity new lives, which must be either a blessing or a curse. But the dignity of such a course is not its only, nor, indeed, its main, recommendation. More important is the absolute necessity that the conditions of the union of the two adult lives should be clearly and thoroughly understood between them. No wise people enter into engagements of an important and durable character without a written agreement; a definite contract excludes all chance of disagreement as to the arrangements made, and prevents misunderstandings from arising. A verbal contract may be misunderstood by either party; lapse of time may bring about partial forgetfulness; slight disagreements may result in grave quarrels. If the contract be a written one, it speaks for itself, and no doubt can arise which cannot be reasonably settled. All this is readily seen where ordinary business partnerships are concerned, but some—unconsciously rebounding from the present immoral system, and plunging into the opposite extreme—consider that the union in marriage of man and woman is too tender and sacred a thing to be thus dealt with as from a business point of view. But it must be remembered that while love is essential to true and holy marriage, marriage implies more than love; it implies also a number of new relations to the outside world which—while men and women live in the world—cannot be wholly disregarded. Questions of house, of money, of credit, &c., necessarily arise in connection with the dual home, and these cannot be ignored by sensible men and women. The contract does not touch with rude hands the sensitive plant of love; it concerns itself only with the garden in which the plant grows, and two people can no more live on love alone than a plant can grow without earth around its roots. A contract which removes occasions of disagreement in business matters shelters and protects the love from receiving many a rude shock. "Society will ere long," said Mr. Conway, "be glad enough to assimilate contracts between man and woman to contracts between partners in business. Then love will dispense alike with the bandage on its eyes and the constable's aid." Some pre-nuptial arrangement seems necessary which shall decide as to the right of inheritance of the survivor of the married pair. As common property will grow up during the union, such property should pass to the survivor and the children, and until some law be made which shall prevent parents from alienating from their children the whole of their property, a provision guarding their inheritance should find its place in the proposed deed. A definite marriage contract is also desirable for the sake of the children who may proceed from the union. Society has a right to demand from those who bring new members into it, some contract which shall enable it to compel them to discharge their responsibilities, if they endeavour to avoid them. If all men and women were perfect, no contract would be necessary, any more than it would be necessary to have laws against murder and theft; but while men and women are as they are, some compulsive power against evil-doers must be held in reserve by the law. Society is bound to guard the interests of the helpless children, and this can only be done by a clear and definite arrangement which makes both father and mother responsible for the lives they have brought into existence, and which shows the parentage in a fashion which could go into a law-court should any dispute arise. Again, if there were no contract, in whom would the guardianship of the children be vested, in case of wrong-doing of either parent, of death, or of separation? Suppose a brutal father: his wife leaves him and takes the children with her; how is she to keep them if he claims and takes them? If she has the legal remedy of divorce, the Court awards her the guardianship and she is safe from molestation. If a wife elope, taking the children with her, is the father to have no right to the guardianship of his sons and daughters, but to remain passive while they pass under the authority of another man? Application for divorce would guard him from such a wrong. If the parents separate, and both desire to have the children, how can such contest be decided, save by appeal to an impartial law? Marriage, as before urged, is a partnership, and where common duties, common interests, and common responsibilities grow up, there it is necessary that either party shall have some legal means of redress in case of the wrong-doing of the other.

To those who, on the other hand, object to facility of divorce being granted at all, it may fairly be asked that they should not forget that to place divorce within the reach of people, is not the same as compelling them to submit to it. Those who prefer to regard marriage as indissoluble could as readily maintain the indissolubility of their own wedded tie under a law which permitted divorce, as they can do at the present time. But those who think otherwise, and are unhappy in their marriages, would then be able to set themselves free. No happy marriage would be affected by the change, for the attainability of divorce would only be welcomed by those whose marriage was a source of misery and of discord; the contented would be no less content, while the unhappy would be relieved of their unhappiness; thus the change would injure no one, while it would benefit many.

It is a pity that there is no way of obtaining the general feminine view of the subject of marriage and divorce; women who study, who form independent opinions are—so far as my experience goes—unanimous in their desire to see the English laws altered; advanced thinkers of both sexes are generally, one might say universally, in favour of change. To those who think that women, if polled to-morrow, would vote for a continuance of the present state of things, may be recommended the following passage from Mrs. Mill: "Women, it is said, do not desire, do not seek what is called their emancipation. On the contrary, they generally disown such claims when made in their behalf, and fall with *acharnement* upon any one of themselves who identifies herself with their common cause. Supposing the fact to be true in the fullest extent ever asserted, if it proves that European women ought to remain as they are, it proves exactly the same with respect to Asiatic women; for they too, instead of murmuring at their seclusion, and at the restraint imposed upon them, pride themselves on it, and are astonished at the effrontery of women who receive visits from male acquaintances, and are seen in the streets unveiled. Habits of submission make men as well as women servile-minded. The vast population of Asia do not desire or value, probably would not accept, political liberty, nor the savages of the forest, civilization; which does not prove that either of those things is undesirable for them, or that they will not, at some future time, enjoy it. Custom hardens human beings to any kind of degradation, by deadening the part of their nature which would resist it. And the case of women is, in this respect, even a peculiar one, for no other inferior caste that we have heard of have been taught to regard their degradation as their honour." Mr. Conway considers that changed circumstances would rapidly cause women to be favourable to the proposed alteration: "Am I told," he remarks, "that woman dreads the easy divorce? Naturally, for the prejudices and arrangements of society have not been adapted to the easy divorce. Let her know that, under the changed sentiment which shall follow changed law, she will meet with sympathy where now she would encounter suspicion; let her know that she will, if divorced from one she loves not, have only her fair share of the burdens entailed by the original mistake; and she who of all persons suffers most if the home be false will welcome the freer marriage" ("The Earthward Pilgrimage," p. 289).

Both in theory and in practice advanced thinkers have claimed facility of divorce. John Milton, in his essay on "Divorce," complains that "the misinterpreting of Scripture . . . hath changed the blessing of matrimony not seldom into a familiar and co-inhabiting mischiefe; at least into a drooping and disconsolate household captivitie, without refuge or redemption" (p. 2), and in his Puritan fashion he remarks that because of this "doubtles by the policy of the devill that gracious ordinance becomes insupportable," so that men avoid it and plunge into debauchery. Arguing that marriage is not to be regarded merely as a legitimate kind of sexual intercourse, but rather as a union of mind and feeling, Milton says: "That indisposition, unfitness, or contrariety of mind, arising from a cause in nature unchangable, hindring and ever likely to hinder the main benefits of conjugall society, which are solace and peace, is a greater reason of divorce than natural frigidity, especially if there be no children, and that there be mutual consent" (p. 5). Luther, before Milton, held the same liberal views. Mary Wolstonecraft acted on the same theory in her own life, and her daughter was united to the poet Shelley while Shelley's first wife was living, no legal divorce having severed the original marriage. Richard Carlile's second marriage was equally illegal. In our own days the union of George Henry Lewes and George Eliot has struck the key-note of the really moral marriage. Mary Wolstonecraft was unhappy in her choice, but in all the other cases the happiest results accrued. It needs considerable assurance to brand these great names with immorality, as all those must do who denounce as immoral unions which are at present illegal.

In the whole of the arguments put forward in the above pages there is not one word which is aimed at real marriage, at the faithful and durable union of two individuals of opposite sexes—a union originated in and maintained by love alone. Rather, to quote Milton once more, is reverence for marriage the root of the reform I urge: he who "thinks it better to part than to live sadly and injuriously to that cherfull covnant (for not to be belov'd and yet retain'd, is the greatest injury to a gentle spirit), he I say who therefore seeks to part, is one who highly honours the married life, and would not stain it; and the reasons which now move him to divorce, are equall to the best of those that could first warrant him to marry" (p. 10). In the advocacy of such views marriage is elevated, not degraded; no countenance is given to those who would fain destroy the idea of the durable union between one man and one woman. Monogamy appears to me to be the result of civilization, of personal dignity, of cultured feeling; loyalty of one man to one woman is, to me, the highest sexual ideal. The more civilized the nature the more durable and exclusive does the marriage union become; in the lower ranges of animal life difference of sex is enough to excite passion: there is no individuality of of choice. Among savages it is much the same: it is the female, not the woman, who is loved, although the savage rises higher than the lower brutes, and is attracted by individual beauty. The civilised man and woman need more than sex-difference and beauty of form; they seek satisfaction for mind, heart, and tastes as well as for body; each portion the complex nature requires its answer in its mate. Hence it arises that true marriage is exclusive, and that prostitution is revolting to the noble of both sexes, since in prostitution love is shorn of his fairest attributes, and passion, which is only his wings, is made the sole representative of the divinity. The fleeting connections supposed by some Free Love theorists are steps backward and not forward; they offer no possibility of home, no education of the character, no guarantee for the training of the children. The culture both of father and of mother, of the two natures of which its own is the resultant, is necessary to the healthy development of the child; it cannot be deprived of either without injury to its full and perfect growth.

But just as true marriage is invaluable, so is unreal marriage deteriorating in its effects on all concerned: therefore, where mistake has been made, it is important to the gravest interests of society that such mistake should be readily remediable, without injury to the character of either of those concerned in it. Freed from the union which injures both, the man and woman may seek for their fit helpmeets, and in happy marriages may become joyful servants of humanity, worthy parents of the citizens of to-morrow. Men and women must know conjugal, before they can know true parental, love; each must see in the child the features of the beloved ere the perfect circle of love can be complete. Husband and wife bound in closest, most durable and yet most eager union, children springing as flowers from the dual stem of love, home where the creators train the lives they have given—such will be the marriage of the future. The loathsome details of the Divorce Court will no longer pollute our papers; the public will no longer be called in to gloat over the ruins of desecrated love; society will be purified from sexual vice; men and women will rise to the full royalty of their humanity, and hand in hand tread life's pathways, trustful instead of suspicious, free instead of enslaved, bound by love instead of by law.